FOUR VIEWS OF CHRIST

Books by Andrew Jukes

Four Views of Christ
The Names of God
The Law of the Offerings
Types in Genesis

FOUR VIEWS OF CHRIST

*Revealing portraits of the life and ministry
of Jesus Christ in the four Gospels*

by
Andrew Jukes

Edited by
James Shiffer Kiefer

kregel PUBLICATIONS

Grand Rapids, MI 49501

Four Views of Christ, by Andrew Jukes, © 1966 by Kregel Publications, a division of Kregel, Inc., P.O. Box 2607, Grand Rapids, Michigan 49501. All rights reserved.

Cover Photo: CLEO Freelance Photography
Cover Design: Alan G. Hartman

Library of Congress Cataloging-in-Publication Data

Jukes, Andrew John, 1815-1901.
    Four Views of Christ

    (Andrew Jukes Reprint Series)
            p.   cm.
    Reprint. Originally published: the Characteristic Differences of the Four Gospels. New York: Revell, 1853.
    1. Bible. N.T. Gospels—Criticism, interpretation, etc.
2. Jesus Christ—Person and offices. I. Kiefer, James Shiffer. II. Bible. N. T. Gospels. English. 1982. III. Title.
IV. Series: Jukes, Andrew John, 1815-1901. Works. 1982.
BS2555.J8   1982   226'.06   82-7800
                                                  AACR2

ISBN 0-8254-2953-6 (pbk.)

        3 4 5 6 7 8 Printing/Year 97 96 95 94 93

Contents

Editor's Note

Not every worthwhile work of previous generations warrants a reprinting today. However, there are yet some that ought to be made available to this present generation of Bible students. I firmly believe that this small book belongs to this latter group.

It would have been possible to make a cheap facsimile edition. However, the archaic expressions were all too frequent, and the system of footnoting rather ponderous. The publisher is to be complimented for investing in editorial work and new type-casting in order to bring this work to you in a form more suitable for the twentieth-century reader.

It is my hope that many will find these pages to be both enlightening and stimulating as the pattern of the four Gospels is made plain.   JSK

Preface

IT IS A MARK of love to dwell on the perfections of a be-loved object, to notice and treasure up tones which fall unheeded on the unloving ear. Love of the truth, where it is deep and real, here resembles other love. It sees beauties where the unloving can discern none. Kings of the Gentiles who come to Zion may pass by together, may see it, and marvel, and hasten away. But he who dwells there will go around about her, and tell her towers; will mark her bulwarks, and count her palaces. His love for his home makes him quick to see its beauties, and to challenge others to notice and admire them with him.

The joy I have had in the study of the Gospels, more es-pecially since through grace the scales fell from my eyes, and I saw in their structure and diversity marks of a Divine purpose, has been such that I could wish to make others partakers with me in it; for to me the discovery of a reason for their form was like the acquiring of a new sense. Since then, as opportunity has served, I have led others to the subject. Recently I delivered the lectures which compose this volume. And now, though with the deepest sense of their imperfectness, I commit them to the press, at the re-peated request of those who heard them. I have rather in-dicated the nature of the subject than sounded its depths. I do not know how far this age is prepared to eat "the hid-den manna." But I shall rejoice if my attempt directs others to a line of truth, which I am sure demands the special at-tention of the Church of today.

For now as ever, though now more keenly, the wisdom of this world is arrayed to prove the wisdom of God to be folly, because He has given His truth in a form, which, though it finds the lost, seems too childish and simple for wise and prudent ones. Only recently I met a man accounted wise in this world who told me, that "the crucial test which had of late been applied to the Gospels had proved them to be very different from the Divine thing which many took them for." I asked him if he knew the story, how, when the Truth came in the flesh, humbling Himself to that form, that thereby He might reach the very lowest, the "crucial test" was tried on Him too, and He was adjudged "a deceiver"; at least so said the men who used the "crucial test." So must the written Word be tried; for disputers of this world still stumble at the human form of the Word, not seeing that it is part of the mystery of the incarnation. But crucial tests, which could not be used against it, if God had not spoken to us in human form, "even as a man speaketh with his friend," will only prove to loving disciples the deeper glory of that Word, which, though Human, is yet Divine.

It only remains for me to acknowledge my many obligations to a beloved friend, whose love and instructions I count among the many blessings God has given me. To a little anonymous volume by him on St. Luke, and a paper on St. Mark, published some years ago in a now defunct periodical, I owe much. I am glad to be his debtor, for I feel that "wherever it can be shown we are not original, so much the better: our desire should be to enter the circle of the great dependence of all things; secure that there is no independence of heart or mind upon any other terms." Only "with all saints" can "we comprehend what is the depth and length" (Eph. 3:18) of that which is presented to us in Christ Jesus. And the household which is too small by itself to take in the whole Lamb, can and must do so by the aid of others. For God will have every part of His Lamb to be apprehended by us, thus by our very weakness linking us to one another.

And now, O Lord, to Thee do I commend this little work. It is nothing with Thee to help with few or many. My feebleness cannot hinder if Thou wilt work. Work Thou to Thine own glory.

Four Views of Christ

"A river went out of Eden, to water the garden, and from thence it was parted, and became into four heads." —GEN. 2:10.

"The first living creature was like unto a Lion; the second living creature was like unto a Calf; the third living creature had a face as a Man; the fourth living creature was like a flying Eagle." —REV. 4:7.

Introduction

"A river went out of Eden, to water the garden, and from thence it was parted, and became into four heads" GEN. 2:10.

WE ARE TOLD OF ST. AUGUSTINE that on one occasion when his mind was much engaged in the contemplation of the doctrine of the Trinity, he was walking by the sea, and saw a child filling a shell with the water, which he then carried and poured into a hollow in the sand. "What are you doing, my boy, with that water?" said the Saint. "I am going to put all the sea into this hole," replied the child. The Father smiled and passed on, when a voice seemed to say to him, "And thou too art doing the like, in thinking to comprehend the depths of God in the narrow limits of thy finite mind."

The attempt to treat of the differences of the Gospels within a few brief lectures, may appear to be only a repetition of the child's attempt to drain the sea. But I make no such attempt. I bear a cupful of water, a taste of what is at hand for all who seek and wait to draw it, not that, like Ishmael, any should be content to go forth with but a bottle; for in the dry and thirsty land, if our water is only in bottles, it will soon be all consumed; but rather to lead men like Isaac to dwell by the well, knowing that never is the water so sweet to us as when we draw it ourselves fresh from the living fountain.

Those who, like Ishmael, trust to bottles are not only oft-times faint, but have no eye for the well, which, though they see it not, springs close to them even in the dreary land. But the elect dwell by the waters, and open wells while others stop them, that man and beast may drink

11

thereat. If in a day when the human mind seems more than ever alive to extract every possible refreshment from the streams of this world, I can point to a better spring — if, in a word, by the examples given here, I may lead some to the Gospels, prayerfully and humbly to wait there for the streams of God, these pages will not be in vain. I should be happy if the joy my own soul has had in the study could be communicated to others into whose hands this little book may come.

To speak then of the Gospels. As every one knows, there are four. By many these are regarded as merely supplementary or corroborative of one another. That they serve this end, as coincident testimonies, I do not doubt. But this is secondary, the chief purpose being, I am sure, the revelation of the Lord in certain distinct relationships. Even an ordinary man's life might be written thus: one biographer giving his public, another his private and more domestic life. One would select one class of facts: another, omitting these, would record others, as better suiting his own purpose. Indeed, given the self-same facts, the two would notice different circumstances, without making either narrative imperfect in the particular view in which it was composed. It is just so in the Gospels. Each has its own purpose: each, therefore, has its own peculiar selection and arrangement of facts recorded.

An example may illustrate this. Take, then, the life of Napoleon. If I wished to show his skill as a military commander, I might select some word or deed of boldness in the field. Did I wish to show his kind-heartedness, I might simply quote a letter written after the battle, sympathizing with the sorrows of one whose friend or brother had fallen. With another view I might point to the *Despatches,* so clear and true, as illustrative of the literary ability of the same person. Thus from the self-same scene I might make selections of the circumstances to record, according to the particular end which I had before me in my writing. And also the order of the events narrated. If my purpose is to show the progress of a certain course of action, chronological order must be adhered to accurately. On the other hand, if I only wish to illustrate the spirit and character of that action, in which various facts all speak the same language, chronological order may be dispensed with without error. In each case the one question is, What is the writer's purpose? Unless this is understood, the writing will fail to accomplish in us its specific end however instructive it may be.

Take again the *Code Napoleon* as an example. If I should speak of it as a monument of the genius of him whose name it bears, I might select particular parts in which the bearing of law on society, an intuitive perception of just results in details, and the vast scope of design, were manifest, and show that these originated in his mind. If another history should seek to show Napoleon's own power in employing instruments, it might show the very same parts drawn up by men able in their vocation; and a caviller might find difficulty to reconcile the drawing up of all of them with the originating mind which had set all going and directed it throughout. Were I showing the progress of legislation in the world, I might allege these very same parts as the necessary consequence of the progress of society, and that they flowed as the obvious consequences from the preceding steps in this process, as one idea leads on to another; and, in appearance, Napoleon's originality would disappear.

All these histories might be true, yet seem impossible to one who had only these to reconcile them in everything; because he has not the additional elements and a knowledge of the whole order of man's mind and history, which would be absolutely necessary to put them together. Is God's history of His Son in the world less vast in conception, less multifarious in the relationships it speaks of, than Napoleon and a code of laws?

And yet many speak of Holy Scripture as if its form were accidental, without a thought whether such a supposition be worthy or unworthy of a Divine revelation. Ignorant of God and His purpose and laws, they do not hesitate to judge His Word. To act thus with heathen poets, and charge them with ignorance, because the form of their verse is unlike ours, would of course be great presumption. But to judge God's Word without having His Spirit is to rely on the world's wisdom, and that is still utter foolishness. For the secret of the Lord is with them that fear Him. In His sanctuary some have learned to admire the grace and wisdom of this His revelation; and having given Him credit for having an object in its form have in due time learned by His Spirit what the object is. They know, as one of old expressed it, that "the living Word, humbling Himself to come in human form, became all things to all men, in a more Divine sense than St. Paul, in order that thus He might win all men."*

The human form, therefore, of the Written Word to them is no stumbling-block. They see that it is but part and parcel of the mystery of the Incarnation. They know, too, even though the world does not, that the division of Scripture into books, in each of which some particular aspect of the elect's position, and of God's grace to meet it, is given to us, was thus appointed the better to reveal Him, by dividing His light as with a prism, here a little and there a little, as man could bear it.

In Paradise this might not be needed. There man might better conceive of God. But though in Eden the river of the water of life flowed in one full stream, when it left the Garden, and went forth into the world, it was seen parted into several channels. Could we comprehend Christ as He is, we should not need the many streams; but, being where and what we are, this form of the revelation is very gracious; a witness among many, that the "sundry times and divers manners" of the communication were all additional expressions of perfect love.

The fact is that our perceptions do not grasp realities, but their forms. If therefore what is seen is to be described, we must have many representations even of the same ob-

---

* Origen, *Comment. in Johan.* Vol. x.

ject; and this not only because the same object may be viewed on different sides, but because the amount of what is seen even on the same side will depend on the light and capacity of the beholder. He who made us knew this and provided for it. Hence of old, in type and figure, we have view after view of Him who was to come; not only because His offices and perfections were many, but also because we were weak and needed such a revelation.

Thus in the single relation of offering, Christ is seen a Burnt-offering, Peace-offering, and Sin-offering, each but a different view of the same one offering; each of which again may be seen in various measures, and yet the offering itself is only one. And just as in the self-same act of dying on the cross, our Lord was at the same moment a sweet-savor offering, willingly offering to God a perfect obedience, and also a sin-offering, penally bearing the judgment due to sin, and as such made a curse for us;* so in the selfsame acts of His life, each act may be seen in different aspects, for each act has a Divine fulness. It is this fulness which God in mercy presents to our view in the diversities of the Four Gospels.

It is for this reason that a Harmony of the Gospels, though it is interesting and has its uses, leads us from the special purpose for which the Gospels were written as they are. For by arranging everything chronologically many passages lose the force which they possess as portions of a distinct series. Here in historic, there in moral order, the Spirit of God has put this or that fact touching the Son before me. The facts are precious, get them as I may, but they are doubly precious if I am able to apprehend the purpose of

---

* For those not familiar with the typical offerings, I may note here that in "the sweet-savour offerings," man came to present an offering, which, as a sweet feast to God, was consumed upon His altar. In "the sin-offerings," man came as a sinner, and his offering, as charged with sin, was cast out, and burnt, not on the altar, but on the ground "without the camp." In the one the offerer came as an accepted worshipper: in the other as a condemned sinner. See Lev. 1-5. Both views meet in the death of Christ.

God in presenting them in this or that relation. Then each scene, in its omissions, in its form, in its position in the series, is part of a Divine mystery, which, though hid from the wise and prudent of the world, is yet often revealed to babes by the Holy Spirit.

The early Church saw this. And with one voice they testify to what they saw, namely, that the Four Gospels contained four different aspects of the Great Manifestation. And though to say that the Fathers so viewed the matter may not in these days commend the view, it will at least prove that the doctrine here is no novelty. The emblem which they applied to the Gospels was that of the Four Cherubim or "living creatures," conceiving that these four "living creatures" were apt representations of the Four Evangelists or Gospels, or rather, more correctly to express their thought, of those manifestations of Christ Himself which the Four Gospels respectively present to us, Christ himself being one and the same in each, yet seen and set forth by each in a different aspect. Illuminated missals, old Bibles, and the windows of Churches, in which these cherubic forms are connected with the Four Evangelists, show that, right or wrong, the Church for centuries has regarded this as a correct application. I believe they were right, and I am content to take the same symbols, finding no others which so well express the general and particular character of each and all the Gospels.

And here, though what I contend for is not the symbol but the fact, it may be well to show in what way the symbol of the Cherubim can be connected with certain views of Christ's person. For some may ask, Are not the Cherubim angels? If I err not, the Cherubim are always the Divine in creature form, the vessel in or by which the Lord reveals His glory. If He shows Himself in angels, then so far angels may be Cherubim. If He shows Himself in "living creatures full of eyes," who say, "Thou hast redeemed us,"* then the redeemed are Cherubim. The Jews say that the

---

* Cf. Rev. 4:8; 5:8, 9.

Cherubim in the temple were the memorials of God's descent at the giving of the Law. That descent on Mount Sinai was a manifestation, even if "by the disposition of angels" (Acts 7:53), of His glory. But that descent, though the Jews never understood it, was itself a pledge of another and greater, when He who then wrote His laws on stone would write them in flesh, and descend to show His glory in the only begotten Son.

For my own part, without pretending fully to explain "the living creatures," I cannot doubt that they are a vessel to reveal the Lord's glory; as such linked to the manifestation made in the flesh of Christ, and again that which shall be made in His mystic body, the Church of the redeemed first-born. For the one fore-shadows the other. And just as the work of the potter, before it feels the fire, has on it all those lines of beauty which shall be seen when the vessel has passed through the furnace, though none but the potter's eye can as yet trace the beauty; so do the Gospels contain hidden within them figures, not only of the revelation once made in Christ, but of that far more wondrous one which shall be made when the kingdom now in mystery shall be revealed openly. But on this I cannot enter here. Enough if I have shown on what grounds "the living creatures" may be used as figures of the various aspects of the manifestation given us in Christ Jesus.

As to details, the figures are these: "The first living creature was like unto a lion; the second living creature was like unto a calf; the third living creature had a face as a man; and the fourth living creature was like a flying eagle" (Rev. 4:7). The four camps in the wilderness — the camp of Reuben, of Judah, of Ephraim, and of Dan — had, it is said, these four figures on their respective standards:* for Israel was the elect vessel in which the Lord would be seen; on them, therefore, in a way they little thought, was stamped some figure of that which should one day be seen

---

* Num. 2. Jewish tradition declares that Reuben's standard was the man, Judah's the lion, Ephraim's the ox, Dan's the eagle.

in the true Israel (Isa. 49:3, 4). And in every age the lion, and ox, and man, and eagle, have all been seen in some part of the camp of the saints or the beloved city.

Of the meaning of the figures I need scarely speak. If Christ is seen as "the lion," a heavenly voice tells us in what connection He holds this form: "The lion of the tribe of Judah is the root of David"(Rev. 5:5; 22:16), again: "Judah is my lawgiver"(Psa. 108:8). Under this figure, therefore, I expect to find Him as a Son of Abraham, connected with a kingdom, and so with Abraham's seed. Then as to "the calf." This is the figure for service. So we read, "Thou shalt not muzzle the mouth of the ox that treadeth out the corn" (I Cor. 9:9), and again: "Much increase is by the strength of the ox" (Prov. 14:4). Under this figure I expect to see the Lord as the patient laborer for others, if need be offering Himself in His service as a perfect sacrifice. The "man" needs no comment. "The face of a man" bespeaks human sympathy, as it is written, "I drew them with the cords of a man, with bands of love" (Hos. 11:4). Here we shall see the "Son of man," one who can have compassion on the ignorant, seeing He also is compassed with infirmities; who, inasmuch as the children were partakers of flesh and blood, Himself likewise took part of the same; who took not on Him the nature of angels, but who took on Him the seed of Abraham, and was in all points tempted like as we are, yet without sin; that He might be a merciful and faithful High Priest, to make reconciliation for the sins of the people.

Very different is "the eagle." Its ways are above the earth: "the way of an eagle in the air," says the wise man, "is too wonderful for me" (Prov. 30:17-18). Much on the wing, it often rises where no human eye can follow, and possesses the power of gazing with undazzled eyes upon the mid-day sun. Here, "the Word who was with God," who came to reveal the Father, is seen as the One who is from heaven, and whose home is there.

Now those who have most learned Christ, have universally recognized these differing views of Him in the Four Gospels. For love is quick-sighted, and delights to dwell on the peculiarities and perfections of a beloved object. But with the exception of St. John's Gospel, where no question can arise, Christians have differed as to the particular view set forth in each Gospel. The most common view, which has been sanctioned by the Church of Rome, following Jerome and Ambrose and other Fathers, is that which makes the Four Gospels correspond with the order of the Cherubic faces, as seen in Ezekiel's first vision (Ezek. 1:10); that is, first the man, then the lion, then the ox, then the eagle. There is little to recommend this view, except the fact that in Ezekiel's first vision the Cherubic faces are seen in this order. Some, among whom is Augustine, dissent; seeing the man in St. Mark, and the ox in St. Luke, while the lion and the eagle are the aspects he traces respectively in St. Matthew and St. John's Gospels. Others, while agreeing with Augustine in his view of St. John and St. Matthew, see more clearly the ox or service in St. Mark, and the Son of Man in St. Luke's Gospel. I believe the true order is set forth in the vision of St. John, that is, first the lion, then the ox, then the man, and last the eagle.

But whence comes this difference of opinion? The reason is plain. In Ezekiel's vision of the living creatures, each one had all the four faces. And though I am sure that each Gospel has one more special aspect, yet each will give some traits of all the aspects to those who have eyes; while to those who have no eyes, or only half-opened ones, it will present something of all the four together. A distant view of a building often confuses its different sides.

Imperfect views of Christ's offering continually unite or confuse its different aspects, mixing the sin of it with what was a sweet savor; while on the other hand a more perfect comprehension shows many views in each aspect; either of which causes will account for the difference of judgment here. And as to the various views of St. Mark, where one sees the man, others the ox, a special reason may be found in St. Paul's words, "He took upon Him the form of *a servant*, and was made in the likeness of *men*" (Phil. 2:7). The one relation is so close to the other, that one runs into the other: one therefore very easily may be substituted or mistaken for the other. For as it is said of the living creatures, "two wings of every one were joined one to another," so in certain places the view peculiar to one Gospel seems to run into another view. And so as to St. Luke. I can quite understand how, seeing the special mercy there to the lost, some have connected this Gospel with the idea of atonement, and taken "the ox," the sacrificial animal, as an emblem of it. Nevertheless I feel certain that, according to the order of the living creatures in St. John's vision, the third Gospel shows "the man"; that it is as man that Christ meets the lost — "the priest must be taken from among men" (Heb. 5:1, 2); — as man He makes the atonement. And the following pages will show why I prefer the view which regards St. Luke's Gospel as the revelation of the Son of Adam. At the same time, while I see how "they four had one likeness" (Ezek. 10:10), I am not surprised that men with different feelings have differed here.

The old tradition as to the Lord, that He appeared very different to different men, seems to me in point here, and quite probable. For something of this sort must be true of the Word in all His manifestations. Take an instance from the written Word. Paul saw in Hagar and Sarah what an unbeliever could not see. I look into the Gospels: how infinitely different do they appear to me, and to the sceptic who only sees in them certain exploded myths; and yet how very far does my view come short of that of angels and saints within the veil. So with the formed Word of creation; "the heavens which declare His glory"; how different is it to a Newton and to a New Zealand savage! So with the Word made flesh. To one He is but as "a root out of a dry ground"; to another He is "the chiefest among ten thousand, and altogether lovely." It is so on all points. The Word must appear different to different men, because each sees, and can only see, with his own measure, and from his own standpoint.

And this leads me to notice the writers of the Gospels; for the view of each is wonderfully connected with his own

character. Each sees from his own ground. Matthew, a
Jew and publican, one who, though by birth an Israelite,
by his office as publican had been an official of the Roman
empire, and so had been accustomed to contemplate a vast
kingdom, sees our Lord both as Son of Abraham and of
David, connected with Abraham's seed, and also with a
kingdom. Mark was the Apostle's servant: "They had John,
whose surname was Mark, for their minister" (Acts 12:12);
and Paul says of him, "Take Mark, and bring him with thee,
for he is profitable to me for the ministry." This is the man,
living to serve, who sees the Lord as Servant; his own service being probably, not only the result of what he had seen
in the Lord, but also a means for better enabling him to
appreciate the perfections of that blessed ministry. Luke,
apparently a Gentile, as he is distinguished by St. Paul
from "those of the circumcision," the friend and companion of Paul, the Apostle of the Gentiles, whose ministry re-
spected neither Jew nor Gentile, but addressed itself to man
as such, is the one who sees Christ as the Son of Adam or
Son of Man, not so much connected with a kingdom, or the
Servant of God, as the One whose sympathies as a Man
linked Him with Adam's fallen and ruined children.

John, who leaned on the bosom of His Lord, sees Him
as the Son in the bosom of the Father, not of the world,
though for a season in it, to draw a heavenly people up-
ward from it to the Father's house above. In each case the
vessel used by the Spirit was fitted for the special task.
He knew, if they did not, His own purpose in thus variously
tuning His chosen instruments. The result is full harmony
to the instructed ear. I know that some, who have pre-
sumed to judge here after the flesh, complain of dissonance.
I know, too, that to the savage ear our full chord is con-
fused and strange; and how a note which seems like a dis-
cord could add character and tone, would be utterly in-
comprehensible. But the harpist, whose music satisfies the
instructed, can afford to be judged by the untaught. The
Lord did not lack perfectness, because some on earth saw
no beauty in Him that they should desire Him.

I would yet add a word as to the order of the Gospels, for I am certain that the order of Scripture, as we now have it, involves deep teaching. Here as well as in all other things God has had a hand. And indeed it needs no special light to see that in the Four Gospels, the character of the revelation increases in depth, or at least changes its form, as we proceed. The first thousand cubits the waters were to the ankles; the second thousand cubits the waters were to the knees; the third thousand cubits the waters were to the loins; afterwards it was waters to swim in, a river which could not be passed over.

The King is the first view we get of the Lord. The Son of David is head of a kingdom, of which we all are, or should be, subjects. In this relation He gives His commands, repealing old laws with His, "I say unto you"; while (for His kingdom is one of grace) He invites the weary to come unto Him, and He will give them rest. At the same time, like a righteous judge, He utters the woes which must ensue upon contempt or rejection of His rightful claim. All this we get in St. Matthew; and this is ever the view which an awakened soul first gets of the Lord Jesus.

Soon I get a further view. I see that in His love this Lord has actually become for us a true Servant; not only that He has given commands, but that He has Himself toiled for us. How He toiled comes out with wondrous beauty in the second Gospel. Soon we see even further; not only that He has served, but that verily and indeed He took our place and became a Man for us; a wailing child, bound with swaddling clothes, under human restraints, obeying parents; and then, oh wondrous vision! that He is the heavenly One, the Son of man in heaven. He grows as we look upon Him. Like the vine seen by Pharaoh's butler, which, as he looked, "was as though it budded, and shot forth, and bore clusters" (Gen. 40:10). Christ grows before those who see Him; one relation after another comes out, and comes out, I believe, very much according to the order of these Gospels.

I am sure that in the books of the Old Testament the

order is most marked. We first see what comes out of Adam, the different forms of life growing out of the root of "old Adam." This is the book of Genesis. Then we see that, be it good or bad which has come out of Adam, there must be redemption: so an elect people by the blood of the Lamb are saved from Egypt. This is the book of Exodus. After redemption is known, we come to the experience of the elect, as needing access, and learning the way of it, to God the Redeemer in the sanctuary. This we get in Leviticus. Then in the wilderness of this world, as pilgrims from Egypt, the house of bondage, to the promised land, the trials of the journey are learnt, from that land of wonders and of man's wisdom and art, to the land flowing with milk and honey. This is the book of numbers.

Then comes the desire to exchange the wilderness for the better land, from entering which for a season after redemption is known the elect yet shrink; answering to the desire of the elect at a certain stage to know the power of the resurrection, to live even now as in heavenly places. The rules and precepts which must be obeyed, if this is to be done, come next. Deuteronomy, a second giving of the law, a second cleansing, tells the way of progress. After which Canaan is indeed reached: we go over Jordan: we know practically the death of the flesh, and what it is to be circumcised, and to roll away the reproach of Egypt. We know now what it is to be risen with Christ, and to wrestle not with flesh and blood, but with principalities and powers in heavenly places. This is Joshua. Every instructed Christian has felt this progress; and the books, and their order answer exactly to it.

And so it is, I believe, with the Four Gospels. Nor here only. There is Divine order and progress, I am assured, in the Epistles. There is first Paul's truth, then James's truth, then Peter's truth, and then John's truth:* the same

---

* The thought that Peter and John are types of different forms of Christian life is very common in the old writers; John being taken as the type of the life which is by vision of Christ; Peter, of that life which is by faith and conflict. See Augustine, *Hom. in Johan.* 124.

truth in substance, but given in different forms, meeting the advancing needs of God's elect people. Few now ever really get beyond Paul's form, the first side of truth, giving the first aspect of the application of heavenly mysteries. We are more at home in his arguments, addressed not a little to the mind, than in some of John's simple testimonies. As a proof of this I may say, that for one comment on St. John's Epistles, we have twenty on St. Paul; and this, not because the latter is the most difficult, but because he is more on ground where intellect can find its own. John's line of things in his Epistle is in its simplicity beyond us, even as his Gospel (if indeed Christians knew what it spoke) is not so near and easily comprehended as the view of a kingdom, and that we, with Christ, are members of it. But on this too I forbear: nevertheless the subject will repay the fullest meditation.

But some may ask, Where is the proof that this difference really exists? May I answer, proof is not so much needed as an opened eye. The Jews of old asked signs, instead of the removal of the veil. They could see no proof that Christ was a Divine Person. In questions of sensual things, the senses will yield the proof. Sense proves that fire is hot, and ice cold. Intellect is needed to receive intellectual proof. The senses will not prove a mathematical proposition. To feel as a man, you must be a man, and to feel and see with God, you must possess God's Spirit. "Who knoweth the things of man, save the spirit of man? So the things of God knoweth no man but the Spirit of God" (I Cor. 2:11).

And this is my answer here. Truth is revealed only to the true. The pure in heart, and they only, shall see God. The impure will see the world, or themselves, or their sins. Holiness is needed, if we would see the Lord. Barnabas, who was so surnamed by the Apostles, because he was "a son of consolation," when he came to the brethren at Antioch, "saw in them the grace of God; for," adds the inspired penman, "he was a good man, and full of the Holy Ghost" (Acts 11:23). Pilate, had he gone thither, would never have seen the same. And so of the Gospels. Like the book of nature, they are "the open secret"; open to all, but opened only to a few. Like the holy city, though the gates shall not be shut at all by day, and there is no night there, yet shall there in no wise enter in thither anything that defileth or maketh a lie, but they that are written in the Lamb's book of life. The nations of them that are saved shall walk in the light. By such, the proof, when it is submitted to them, will, I am assured, not be judged lacking. But, oh! how few consider what a tale is told in what we see! how few remember that by it, like the mariner on the ocean, we may find out where we really are!

There is yet another question. Granting the proof, what is the use? What is gained by seeing these distinctions? Such a question — alas! too common — only shows where many now are, and how little God's secrets are prized and treasured by us. Is it nothing to increase in the knowledge of Him, whom to know is life eternal, and "through the knowledge of whom are given to us all things that pertain to life and godliness" (II Peter 1:3)? Shall earthly objects attract, and ignorance be accounted shame, and is it no shame that we so little apprehend the wonders of this blessed revelation? If it be true, too, that "we shall be like Him, when we see Him as He is," is it no gain to grow in intelligent knowledge of Him? He that has seen the great sight will not ask, What is the use? He has seen and believed, and all questioning ends in worship and adoring praise.

The fact is, we need an object. God knows this, though we forget it. He knows that to this day the color of the flocks is changed by the rods put before their eyes in their drinking-troughs (Gen. 30:37). He knows that, in spite of our boastings, the creature cannot be self-existent or self-supported. He therefore gives an object — a revelation of Himself — by the contemplation of which we may rise out of self to bear His image. And just as this revelation is permitted to reach us, it impresses us. We are like Him, when we see Him as He is. But the god of this world, knowing well how the vision of God will transform the creature, strives by another vision, of the glory of this world, to "blind the minds of them which believe not lest the light of the gospel of Christ, who is the image of God, should shine unto them (II Cor. 4:4). But the pure in heart see God. And, such as see Him are changed from grace to grace, into the same image. Let but the light shine on them, and like the moon they must reflect it. The very pool in the street will flash back the rays of heaven, if they do but fall upon it. And we all, "with open face beholding as in a glass the glory of the Lord, are changed into the same image from glory to glory, even as by the Spirit of the Lord" (II Cor. 3:18).

But there is another answer. The Church, as Christ's body, must set Him forth. She is called to be His letter of recommendation before a world that knows Him not (II Cor. 3:3). In her relations to those who are the seed of Abraham, and yet not all children, "for in Isaac shall the seed be called"; in her relation as the Lord's servant in ministry here — in her relation to Adam's seed, or all mankind — in her relation to the heavenly family — is there nothing she has to learn? Those who know the most feel how much instruction they yet need in each and all these relations. Very blessed is it to see how Christ once filled them; for "as He is, so are we in this world." Who has had his eyes in any measure opened to the state of the professing Church — of that body which calls itself, and in one sense is, the seed of Abraham, and the Lord's kingdom — who has not felt the need of special teaching how he should walk towards it? This teaching will be found in that Gospel which shows Christ in connection with the kingdom and with Abraham's seed.

Again, in a day like the present, when so many new philanthropies are being forged to renovate and save a groaning world, is it nothing to have before us the details of that service by which, as God's Servant, our Lord perfectly pleased and glorified Him that sent Him? But every question on this head may be fully answered, as we contemplate the Gospel dedicated to reveal the service of the

Lord's Servant. Again, we are Adam's sons: we are in the world as well as in the Church: we have a link which binds us to all mankind. Is it nothing to know how far that relationship should hold us — how we should sit and walk with publicans and among lost sinners? I look in St. Luke, and I see a Man, in every stage of life, meeting all men, and yet in all well-pleasing to God.

And so of the Son of God, the begotten of the Father. We, too, as His begotten, have a place in His bosom, called to rise above the earth; as such, to be misunderstood and rejected here, and yet while judged, by a heavenly life to be continually judging things around us. Do I want to know the rule here, how, as son of God, Passovers, Sabbaths, and feasts of Tabernacles, may be all fulfilled in me? I look in St. John, and I receive the answer. Oh! for grace, more grace, to walk something more like that most blessed Pattern. In such a walk the world will see nothing — it saw no glory in the Lord. What was there in His relation to the Kingdom, or in His Service, or in His walk as a Man, or as the Son of God, worth noticing? The world saw no beauty. It will see none in us, and yet another Eye shall see the earnest of glory and of everlasting joys.

There is, however, a misuse, as well as a use, of this truth. Intellect may be exercised without conscience. Truth may be used to exalt self, (what is there the flesh will not spoil?) and so bring upon its possessor a worse judgment. Nothing really profits but what sanctifies and humbles. If, like Judas, we use the Word, or our knowledge of Him of whom it testifies, to minister to self, better would it be had we never known Him. If, on the contrary, in the midst of weakness, we use His glorious likeness to humble us for the little measure in which we are as yet conformed to it, and by that Pattern judge in us all which is unlike Him, our knowledge of Him, and His glory, shall not be wholly vain. May these pages, through His grace, serve this end in us! Amen.

Matthew's View

"The first living creature was like unto a Lion" REV. 4:7.
"The Lion of the tribe of Judah hath prevailed to open the book"
REV. 5:5

I HAVE SAID THAT EACH of the Gospels serves a special end, and that the view which is given by St. Matthew of our Lord represents Him in connection with a certain kingdom: that He is not here the Servant of our need, or the Son of Adam, or of God, so much as the Seed of Abraham and Heir of an elect kingdom. The peculiarities of this Gospel will prove this. These peculiarities I would now note as illustrating the special path of the Lord as Son of Abraham. I may then show how these peculiarities give us the special teaching which we need, as to our position as members of a kingdom, and as Abraham's seed. For "as He is, so we are in this world." "He that saith he abideth in Him, ought himself so to walk even as He walked."

First, then, as to what is distinctive. Here the difficulty is selection, for it would far exceed my limits were I to notice every minute point in which St. Matthew differs from the other Gospels. And yet the minute and less marked peculiarities, to the instructed eye, are as striking, and full of import, as those which are greater and more obvious. To my mind, these minor points attest a Divine purpose through the book far more wonderfully than the broad distinctions which no one can overlook. And though an exercise of soul is surely needed to discern them aright, even as there must be an opened ear to hear that voice which in creation, "without speech or language," is ever speaking

29

to us; yet to the humble, light shall not be wanting to show the wisdom of that revelation, which, without a formal declaration of its purpose, can and does reveal that purpose to such as wait on God.

I turn to the Gospel. Its opening verse is at once characteristic. This is "the book of the generation of Jesus Christ, the son of David, the son of Abraham." Here He is Heir of a kingdom, and one of a chosen seed; and so His genealogy is traced through the line of Israel's kings as far as Abraham, and no further. In St. Luke it is traced to Adam; but here it is the Son of Abraham, not of Adam, whom God reveals to us. For an Heir had been promised, and here our Lord is shown as the One in whom the promise of the kingdom was to be fulfilled. The "sure mercies of David" spoke of a kingdom. The covenant ran thus: "I have found David my servant, with holy oil have I anointed him; also I will make him my first-born, higher than the kings of the earth: my mercy will I keep with him for evermore, and my covenant shall stand fast with him: his seed also will I make to endure for ever, and his throne as the days of heaven" (Ps. 80:20-29). Here the Heir is come, and His lineage is given, not as God's or Adam's but as David's Son.

Then in this genealogy four women are mentioned,* each of whom in her life and course had been an appointed figure of the mystery of the kingdom. To see this may need some spiritual discernment; but, seen or unseen, it remains the same. It may not be out of place here, — for few regard these things, — to show how full of teaching is a single

---

* Chap. 1:3, 5, 6. Chrysostom, in his Homilies on St. Matthew, thus introduces this question: — "It is worth inquiry, wherefore can it be that, when tracing the genealogy through the men, he hath mentioned women also; and why, since he determined to do so, he hath yet not mentioned them all, but, passing over the more eminent, such as Sarah, and Rebekah, and as many as are like them, has brought forward them that are famed for some bad thing, as, for instance, a harlot, an adulteress, a mother by incest, and a stranger" *Hom.* i. § 14. I quote this passage for the sake of its opening words: "*It is worth inquiring,*" says Chrysostom. I would to God that Christians thought so, and did "*inquire.*"

distinctive word in these Gospels. To speak then of Tamar, the woman first named here. This figure scarcely needs comment; for, as with Sarah and Hagar, the type is most clear. Judah is the line of the kingdom. The sceptre was his (Gen. 49:10). But his seed, for they were born of a Canaanitish mother, were very evil. Then a younger wife, Tamar, is brought in, and given to Judah's sons; but the children of the old wife dislike her, and have no seed by her. They are cut off for their iniquity. Then Judah's wife grows old and dies. After this the seed of the kingdom passes to her who had been rejected by Judah's sons. And by her, through Judah's sin, Judah being all conscious of it, the line of the kingdom passes from his first sons into another channel. Judah, however, rages against the seed; yea, he is ready to burn the mother. But proof is at hand that her fruit, though Judah knows it not, is Abraham's seed. The signet and staff, though Judah may rage, clearly prove the lineage, and in due time the kingdom is established in the hands of the children of the younger wife.

Surely this scarcely needs interpretation. The first wife of Judah, like Hagar in another type, represents the principles of the Jewish church,* by which Judah strove to build up the line of the elect kingdom. But the seed were evil; and though an attempt was made to improve and build up the line, by bringing in the second and younger wife — that is, the spiritual principles of the new dispensation — yet the sons of the first wife would not have it. They turned from it with loathing, refusing to embrace it, for which abomination judgment overtook them. For even of old the spiritual church was offered to the Jew. In prophets and righteous men it came near to them, but they received it not.

---

* Women in the types are *principles*, either good or bad, as Sarah and Hagar; men, the *activities* or *energies* connected with them. For this reason it is that in the Books of Kings, where we are shown all the different forms of Rule to which God's elect may be subject, the mother of each king is always given, as showing from what principles certain forms of Rule proceed.

So Tamar, the younger wife, was rejected. But time goes on. Judah's wife dies. The old dispensation ends; but not before Judah's sons have been cut off by sore judgments. Then by Judah's own fall, and all unknown to him, the seed passes to the younger wife — for "the seed is the word" — and she becomes fruitful. A seed has sprung out of Judah, which, when sprung, Judah judges, not suspecting the true father. Yea, he is ready to destroy it; but proof is at hand that it is Abraham's seed. The signet and the staff, though Judah may rage, clearly prove the lineage of the Church's children. It is throughout a mystery of the kingdom, showing how the line of heirs should change, and, as such, has a place here in the Gospel devoted to show the Lord in connection with the promised kingdom. And the same may be said of the other women here. I do not enter into details, further than to say that in each of them, with some distinctive peculiarities, the same story of the kingdom will be found repeated; showing how the Gentiles (for these women are Gentiles) should obtain the kingdom and continue the line of Abraham's seed.

But to turn from mysteries to what is on the surface. Here, to omit many minor points,[*] the Lord is called "Emmanuel," that is to say, "God with us," — a name, the witness of the covenant with the kingdom, and also with the elect, testifying that He who had redeemed would not forsake His people. When the kingdom seemed in danger, this was the sign that it should not fail — "A Virgin shall conceive and bear a Son, and His name shall be Emmanuel"; while the same name was again but a fulfilment of the general promise to the elect, "I will dwell in you, and I will walk in you." Then in this Gospel alone do we read of One "born king of the Jews." In St. Luke it is, "Good tidings to all people, for to you is born a Saviour." After

---

[*] Such as the fact, that this genealogy is given at Christ's birth, whereas St. Luke connects his with the baptism; — that here it is a descending series, in St. Luke an ascending one; — that this is Joseph's line, while St. Luke, if I mistake not, gives Mary's; all of which, I am certain, is significant.

which St. Matthew records the immediate effects of the
birth of the royal child. To Herod the king it is an alarm-
ing event, and to all Jerusalem with him; while to distant
Gentiles, who come with gifts, it is matter of joy and praise.
The whole scene being in itself a figure of that mystery of
the kingdom which was even now at hand. But even in the
letter the scene is distinctive. The Lord is seen here as the
Heir; and so of Bethlehem it is said here, and no other
Evangelist notes it, "Out of thee shall come a Governor,
who shall rule my people Israel."

In the following chapter "the kingdom of heaven" is an-
nounced. John the Baptist comes preaching "the kingdom,"
saying, "Repent, for the kingdom of heaven is at hand"
(Chap. 3:1, 2). In St. Mark and St. Luke he preaches "the
baptism of repentance for the remission of sins" (Mark 1:
4; Luke 3:3); in substance the same thing, but recorded
under a form of expression suited to the tenor of each respective Gospel. Here, too, St. Matthew, referring to Isaiah,
quotes the words of the prophet, — "The voice of one crying
in the wilderness, Prepare ye the way of the Lord, make
His paths straight," — and then stops; for what remains of
the quotation does not concern Abraham's seed, but rather
the wide out-lying Gentile world.

But for this very reason St. Luke goes on with the quotation, adding, "Every valley shall be exalted, and every
mountain and hill be brought low"; — the distinction between the Jew and Gentile shall be done away, in the common enjoyment of a heavenly kingdom; — "the crooked
shall be made straight, the rough places plain, and all flesh
shall see the Lord's salvation." St. Matthew goes on, "His
fan is in His hand, and He shall thoroughly purge His
floor, and burn up the chaff with unquenchable fire," — language perfectly suited to the Lord of the kingdom, who
"will gather out of His kingdom all that offends, and them
that work iniquity"; but for this very reason omitted by
St. Mark, for that Evangelist's office is to reveal, not so much
the mighty Lord, as the humble Servant.

All this is characteristic, but the general tenor of the chap-

ter still more so. The "kingdom of heaven" is preached,
for the earthly kingdom of Israel is in ruins. Israel's place
is now to repent, and be buried as dead in a mystic grave.
Then the true Heir, "to fulfill all righteousness," comes into
the place of death, that others there with Him by the same
path of humiliation may obtain a better kingdom. Then
"heaven is opened," and the Spirit descends, a witness that
"the kingdom of heaven" is at hand, and that the sons of
Abraham shall be partakers in it. Here this "opening of
heaven" is connected with the announcement of "the kingdom of heaven." But because it has other bearings, on the
service of the elect, and also on the world generally, it finds
its place in the other Gospels which describe the Servant
and the Son of Man: St. Mark speaks of its bearing on
service, for there is no true service until heaven is opened
to us, and the Holy Spirit comes: St. Luke records it as
showing that man enters heaven only by death and resurrection, that for man as man the way of life and peace is
through the flood. Here in St. Matthew, both the "preaching of the kingdom," which is peculiar, and the "opening
of heaven," which is common, are equally characteristic of
the special aim of this Gospel. And most instructive is it
to observe how even what is common to the Gospels, becomes peculiar by its position as part of a distinct series.

Then comes the temptation. The "kingdoms of this
world" are set in array before Him who has received the
testimony of the "kingdom of heaven," and has seen "heav-
en opened." Both St. Matthew and St. Luke record this,
for to Abraham's son, and to man as man, the kingdoms
of this world and their glory are a very special trial. St.
Mark and St. John omit it, as outside their views of Ministry
and of The Word; the omission with them being as characteristic as is the insertion here. This temptation the Heir
of the Kingdom overcomes, after which He comes Himself
preaching the kingdom of heaven. "From that time Jesus
began to preach, and to say, Repent, for the kingdom of
heaven is at hand" (Chap. 4:17).

The next scene, the Sermon on the Mount, is more distinctive. Here, beginning with a beatitude touching "the kingdom," the Lord with authority unfolds the principles and laws, and describes the subjects of His kingdom: not one verse of which, be it observed, is recorded in St. Mark, who, though generally following St. Matthew, invariably omits what is connected with power in the kingdom, as inconsistent with the view which it is his office to present to us.

Here many points are characteristic: the tone of authority throughout: the repeated "I say unto you," where the letter of Moses is set aside to make way for a higher Spirit: the special teaching, too, as to the connection of the Law of Moses with the New Law; how the latter was not to destroy the Law and the Prophets, but to fulfil them: the doxology in the Lord's prayer, with an allusion to "the kingdom," given here but omitted in St. Luke: the repeated reference to a "kingdom," the character of which is remarkably implied in its distinctive title; in other Gospels the "kingdom of God," here only the "kingdom of heaven"; a peculiar expression which occurs near thirty times in this Gospel: so too the marks of His subjects, among which "righteousness" is specially named: — all this, not to speak of other points, is peculiar to St. Matthew, and all characteristic.

As to the "kingdom," and the remarkable fact, that in St. Matthew only it is "the kingdom of heaven," I will speak more fully when I come to notice the special teaching which we get in what is peculiar to this Evangelist. I would, however, beg that it may be noticed that though in three places in this Gospel, the expression, "kingdom of God," occurs, in each case the reason for this variation in the language is obvious, and with a distinct purpose; the "kingdom of heaven" being always the title chosen to mark distinctively what is peculiar to the Lord's kingdom.

And so as to the word "righteousness." To some it may seem trifling to notice that this word occurs frequently in St. Matthew, scarcely ever in the other Gospels. Here it is repeated again and again. "Suffer it to be so now, for thus

it becometh us to fulfill all righteousness" (Chap. 3:15).
"Blessed are they which thirst after righteousness" (Chap.
5:6): "blessed are they which are persecuted for righteousness": — by the way, in St. Luke it is distinctively "reproach
for the Son of Man's sake." So again, "Except your righteousness exceed the righteousness of the Scribes." So again,
"Then shall the righteous shine as the sun in the kingdom of
their Father." So again, "The righteous shall answer, Lord,
when saw we thee an hungered?" So again, "The righteous
into life eternal." So, where in St. Luke it is written, "That
the blood of all the prophets, from the blood of Abel to the
blood of Zechariah, shall be required of this generation";
in St. Matthew we read, "From the blood of righteous Abel
to the blood of Zacharias, whom ye slew between the temple and the altar." So again, where in St. Luke we merely
read, "Seek first the kingdom of God, and all other things
shall be added unto you"; in St. Matthew it is said, "The
kingdom of God, and His righteousness"; righteousness
being a special characteristic of the Lord's kingdom. So St.
Paul teaches, "The kingdom of God is not meat and drink,
but righteousness, and joy, and peace in the Holy Ghost"
(Rom. 14:17). The Gospel of the kingdom peculiarly marks
this, in its notice of "righteousness"; adding also in reference
to peace, "Blessed are the peace-makers"; a beatitude only
to be found in this Gospel.

Having thus published the laws of His kingdom, the Lord
proceeds by acts of grace to bring "the kingdom" nigh to
His elect Israel (Chapters 8-12). And what a kingdom!
The strong man's house is spoiled. Death and disease flee
away before the King's bidding. Lepers are cleansed, the
dead are raised, the storms obey, the devils fear; and yet,
though mercy rejoices against judgment, His people Israel
will not receive their King. Much of this is common to the
other Gospels, for Christ's rejection by the Jew has a bearing both on His course as Servant, and also as showing out
the deceitfulness of the heart of man as man. For which reason many of these scenes are given, with characteristic omissions or additions, both in St. Mark and in St. Luke's Gos-

pels. But here the rejection of the Heir of the Kingdom,
and the nature of His kingdom, are set forth with a fulness
of detail unequalled in any other Gospel.

Of the King Himself St. Matthew tells us, — and the
words are only here, — "Himself took our infirmities, and
bare our sicknesses." Of the spirit of His kingdom, we have
the reiterated witness, "I will have mercy, and not sacrifice"; words, which as they are peculiar to this Gospel, very
distinctly mark the character of that rule which He brought
to sinful men. Then as to His subjects. Only here do we
read, "Many shall come from the east and from the west,
and shall sit down with Abraham, and Isaac, and Jacob,
in the kingdom of heaven. But the children of the kingdom
shall be cast out into outer darkness; there shall be weeping
and gnashing of teeth" (Chap. 8: 11, 12). Israel will not
have Him. Had He come with law, exercising lordship,
He should have been called a benefactor. But because He
comes with grace, to meet the vile, to save the lost, therefore His own receive Him not. Still He preaches "the gospel
of the kingdom," — an expression peculiar to St. Matthew,
— for He is moved with compassion, because they fainted,
and were as sheep having no shepherd. All, however,
whether the Baptist's, His own, or the Apostles' ministry, is
rejected. "He is despised, and they esteem Him not."

Then comes a passage, peculiar to this Gospel, unveil-
ing the heart of the King; in which, while He invites others
to become His subjects, He shows by His own example
what is that kingdom to which He now calls them. He has
come to His own, and they reject Him. Is, then, His kingdom shaken? Nay, but the sin around only the more reveals
that realm of peace, which, like "the brave everlasting firmament," through storms and tempests stood unmoved in
Him.

First, His witness, John, doubts Him; chains and a prison
chill his faith; even as to this hour in days of darkness we
question the very truths, of which in more sunny days we
have been the bold witnesses. Then Israel is like children,
whom no care will please; who will not dance when piped

to, or weep when mourned to. Then the cities which had
witnessed His "mighty works" remain unchanged. Sodom
would have repented; but they repent not. But none of
these things move Him. The Lord of that "kingdom which
is joy and peace," shows that, let what will come from without, there is a kingdom within Him which can overcome
all things. So we read here, — "*At that time* Jesus answered
and said, I thank Thee, O Father, Lord of heaven and earth"
(Chap. 11:25). "At that time," when His servant doubted,
and Israel mocked, and men despised Him; — and who can
tell what hosts of hell by all these circumstances now
pressed against that loving spirit? — "At that time Jesus
answered, I thank thee, Lord. Even so, Father, for so it
seemed good in thy sight." And then at once turning as if
to others, He utters the well-known words, "Come unto me,
all ye that labor, and I will give you rest. Take my yoke
upon you — be now my subjects — and learn of me, for I
am meek and lowly in heart, and ye shall find rest"
(Chap. 11:28, 30).

Here is indeed a kingdom which neither earth nor hell
can move, — "the peace of God which passeth understanding": which can bear all, believe all, hope all, endure all:
which out of apparent defeat can reap yet fresh glories.
Here in the conscious enjoyment of such a kingdom, as now
Lord of all; for it is here, in the midst of this rejection, that
He says, "All things are delivered to me of the Father"
(Chap. 11:27); while yet despised and doubted, He yet
calls us to share His peace, in the kingdom which is not in
creature-blessings, but in the Holy Spirit. This is indeed a
kingdom, to live in the will of God; to understand that will;
to be content with it; — to lose all self-will even in good;
to be glad when self-strength fails; when all self-glorying
is utterly put from us; and yet to joy in God, in that His
will is done, with an unfeigned "Even so, Father, for thus
it pleaseth Thee." Compared with this, what deserves the
name of power or glory? Here is a kingdom worthy of the
high title. Here is victory over all: having nothing, yet
possessing all things: a broken heart, and yet unmeasured

peace. As revealing the kingdom this scene is perfect. As such St. Matthew gives it; while for the same reason it is omitted in the corresponding place in all the other Gospels. The next chapter, (the 12th), though parts of it are common both to St. Mark and St. Luke, becomes generally distinctive by the additions peculiar to this Gospel. The Lord goes through the corn-fields, so choosing the day as to call in question Israel's right to the reality, of which the sabbath had been the appointed token. The omissions or additions of each Evangelist upon this question very clearly mark the distinct and special ends proposed in each narrative. Here we read, "At that time Jesus went on the sabbath through the corn. And the Pharisees said, Behold, thy disciples do that which it is not lawful to do upon the sabbath day. But He said unto them, Have ye never read what David did?" In St. John, under a similar charge, His ground of justification is not "what David did." As Son of the Father the answer is, "My Father worketh hitherto, and I work." In St. Matthew, as Son of David, "what David did" is a fit reply, and characteristic of His position, as coming to His kingdom, and like David at first rejected in it. He thus proceeds, — "Or have ye not read in the law how that on the sabbath days the priests in the temple profane the sabbath and are blameless?" I look to the same scene in St. Luke, but there is not one word there of "priests" or "law"; for there He is Son of Man, on far wider ground, meeting men without law. Then again, here in St. Matthew He adds, "But I say unto you that in this place is One greater than the temple"; words exactly suited by their authority to mark that relation as Lord of the kingdom, which our Lord occupies in this Gospel. I turn to the same scene in St. Mark, and that Evangelist, who up to this point implicitly follows St. Matthew, entirely omits these words, which as being a declaration of kingly power would be out of character in the meek Servant. Finally, here in St. Matthew the Lord repeats, "But if ye had known what this meaneth, I will have mercy and not sacrifice, ye would not have condemned the guiltless"; words to be found in no other Gospel, but very characteristic here, as marking the true nature of the Lord's kingdom.

St. Matthew then proceeds with the tale of rejection, till the Lord withdraws himself, and so acts that the prophecy (St. Matthew alone quotes it), "He shall show judgment to the Gentiles," begins to be accomplished. This Scripture, peculiar to St. Matthew, is again linked with the kingdom. Here we have fresh discoveries of its nature, and glories, and of its rightful Lord. Here only do we read of Him, that "He shall not strive nor cry in the streets; a bruised reed shall He not break, nor quench the smoking flax." For His kingdom is not of this world, but of God, and God is love. It asks not therefore for outward strivings, but rather for silence, and prayer, and quiet contemplation.

The pomp of war, and this world's pride, these and like things men admire. Few believe that humbleness and grace are proofs of true greatness. Men do not see that to come down, one must be high; or that the depth of our descent is the exact measure of our true elevation. But this is seen in the kingdom. There the last is first, and he that has been lowest shall one day be seen highest. St. Matthew, and it is very characteristic, carefully notes this, in these little touches peculiar to him, as affording a lesson respecting the kingdom, much needed even by its true children.

What follows is equally distinctive. These ways strike the crowd. "All the people were amazed, and said, Is not this the Son of David?" St. Luke, the only other Evangelist who records this scene, omits this witness as to "David's Son," telling us simply that "the people wondered." But when the Pharisees heard it they said, "This fellow doth not cast out devils, but through Beelzebub, the prince of the devils." Then the Lord answers again, with two special words, both peculiar to this Gospel, and both distinctive; first declaring, as Lord of the kingdom, "I say unto you, that every idle word which men shall speak, they shall give account thereof in the day of judgment"; and then, that as with the unclean spirit which goes out but returns with seven others worse than the first, "So," — for He speaks as

Judge here, — "shall it be to this wicked generation." After which, renouncing those earthly ties which had bound Him to Israel in the flesh, He acknowledges no other relationship but that of subjection and obedience to the Father's will: — "Whosoever shall do the will of my Father which is in heaven, the same is my brother, my sister, and my mother."

Then comes the unfolding of the mystery of that "kingdom," which should be brought in upon the rejection of the Lord, during His absence for a season growing out of that rejection. This mystery is here opened. The Lord came seeking fruit. He found no fruit in His fig-tree. Then He becomes a Sower. And the history of the period during which He should sit on the Father's throne, until His own throne as Son of Man should be set up, is here given from its first commencement, when the seed was sown in the field, even until the harvest.

This, as it is peculiar to St. Matthew, is quite characteristic. It is true that of these parables, three are given in the other Gospels; St. Mark giving us the Sower and the Mustard-seed, because, though on one side linked with the mystery of the kingdom, they have as manifest a bearing on the path of true service: St. Luke for a like reason giving the same two, and the Leaven also, in an order different from St. Matthew, because the Gentile world is also included in these three parables. St. Luke's order is striking. With him the parable of the Sower stands alone, as an introduction to the three chapters in which he successively describes the preaching, first of the Lord, then of the Twelve, then of the Seventy: while he puts the Mustard-seed and the Leaven, in contrast with the Barren Fig-tree, where he is showing how the Lord, finding no fruit on his fig-tree Israel, on its being cut down should have another tree growing from a little seed, and a leaven of doctrine leavening the whole world. Here in St. Matthew the order is different, for the thing to be unfolded is "the mystery of the kingdom." And distinguishing His disciples from the mass of Israel, as those who through grace were able to understand this mystery, our Lord here unfolds it to them in all its length and breadth. The first parable shows how Christ should now go forth as Sower, and, in spite of Israel's rejection of Him, should yet possess a kingdom. For here in St. Matthew the seed sown is "the word of the kingdom"; in St. Luke it is simply "the word of God." Then come the similitudes of the kingdom. Three spoken to the crowd, describing the outward result of the kingdom, of which all men might take knowledge. The three latter spoken only to the disciples, and descriptive of its true character and value, as seen by those possessing the mind of Christ.

The series as a whole is a complete unfolding of the secret of the kingdom. First the man sows good seed in his field, but his work is soon injured. While men sleep the tares are sown, which, though some would touch them, are spared awhile lest in gathering the tares the wheat be rooted up. Here we have the present state of the world, a mixture of good and bad, which by God's permission is to last until the harvest. Then comes the external form of the kingdom, a vast Gentile thing like Nebuchadnezzar's tree, in which birds of every wing, even those very birds which have plucked away the good seed, can find shelter. Then comes the diffusion of a doctrine through the mass, which the Lord describes as leaven, this also being something visible, inasmuch as the leaven as it spreads would make the meal to rise and work.* All this is outward and visible, and is stated as matter of fact, without bringing in God's estimate of it all, save on this one point, that the tares having been sown are not to be rooted out until the harvest.

Then follow the parables spoken "in the house"; first, of the treasure hid in the field, for the sake of which the field

---

* The word "leaven" I believe is never used in Scripture for what is pure. It is to be remarked that its insertion into the meal is *"the woman's"* work, and not *the man's."* Leaven is sour dough. Whether what is generally spread through Christendom is sweet or sour, a good thing corrupted or a good thing unspoilt, is left for the spiritual intelligence of such as are able to "discern the things that differ."

is bought, though as yet the treasure is not taken out of it; describing (for these last parables give God's view) the value of the Church to Christ, who was content to take the field of this world, for the sake of the treasure hid therein. Then we have the beauty of the treasure, a peerless pearl: Christ's estimate of the loveliness of grace in His redeemed children. Then comes the netful dragged to shore, with the separating process of judgment, the good being gathered and the evil cast away; a view of the judgment, not so much on earth as in heaven; not, as in the Tares, connected with the place where they have grown, but with the place to which those who have been caught in the net must be brought in due season. This subject of itself would fill a volume. Here I only note it as an illustration of the special view of the Lord presented to us in this Gospel.

No less distinctive are the quotations which abound in this Gospel. Again and again we meet the words, "That it might be fulfilled which was spoken by the prophet." The reason is plain. The prophets had spoken of "the kingdom," and the character of its King: therefore are they so carefully quoted in the Gospel of the kingdom. I may note (for this allusion to the prophets is distinctive) some of the Scriptures here quoted, as marking the coming and character of the promised kingdom.

As to the birth of the Heir of the kingdom, it was to be above nature; "that it might be fulfilled which was spoken by the prophet, saying, A virgin shall conceive and bear a Son." The Heir of the kingdom must be begotten of the Holy Spirit. Thus only can we have Emmanuel, that is to say, God with us. As to His acts, "The people in darkness should see great light." "He should take our infirmities, and bear our sicknesses." "He should not strive, nor cry, nor break the bruised reed; but He should send forth judgment unto victory." All this was done "that it might be fulfilled which was spoken by the prophets." And yet when He came to His people, they knew Him not. How this bears on the path of the heirs may perhaps be seen hereafter.

Here I note it as another example of the peculiar tone which runs through this Gospel.

Time would fail me were I to attempt to show how the remainder of this Gospel is to the full as characteristic as that portion over which I have glanced thus hastily. To speak only of its many Parables. With, I think, three exceptions, each of which is significant, they are all similitudes of "the kingdom of heaven." We have seen how "the kingdom of heaven is like unto leaven," "the kingdom of heaven is like a net," "the kingdom of heaven is like unto a merchantman seeking goodly pearls." To the end it is still "the kingdom."

Even in the exceptions I have referred to — namely the Sower, the Two Sons, and the Vineyard, which, as they describe a state of things previous to the setting up of "the kingdom of heaven," could not present similitudes of it* — there is in each an allusion to "the kingdom." The seed of the Sower was "the word of the kingdom." The son, "who said, I will not, but repented and went," is the publican and harlot, who will "go into the kingdom," before those "who said, I go, Sir, but went not." And in the case of the Vineyard, after the husbandmen have killed the Heir, it is added, "Therefore shall the kingdom of God be taken from you, and given to another nation." By the way, observe here it is "the kingdom of God" which is taken from the Jews, not "the kingdom of heaven." They had "the kingdom of God," for they owned God as their king, but they never had "the kingdom of heaven," that form of the kingdom of

---

* These three parables, the Sower, (chap. 13) the Two Sons, (chap. 21:28) and the Vineyard, (chap. 21:33) all represent things prior to the setting up of the kingdom of heaven. The Lord came as "Sower," before He ascended up on high, and thus before the establishment of the heavenly kingdom. The "Two Sons," too, are a figure of man as such, neglecting or giving heed to natural conscience or God's word, all which preceded the coming of the heavenly kingdom. In like manner the letting out of "the Vineyard" to the Jews preceded the rising of the King to heaven. For this reason, none of these three could be similitudes of "the kingdom of heaven."

God which was subsequent to Christ's resurrection into the heavens, and which is the peculiar distinction of this dispensation.° Thus in St. Matthew the burden of the Parables is throughout "the kingdom." The later ones especially reveal this in their whole character. In no other Gospel do we find such words as these, "Then shall the King say to them on His right hand"; and again, "The King shall answer and say, Depart, ye cursed."

How different all this is in St. Luke, must have been observed by every reader. There, in the Gospel of the Son of Man, the peculiar form for beginning a parable is, "A certain man" did this or that; and this invariably. "A certain man had a fig-tree": "a certain man had two sons": "there was a certain rich man who fared sumptuously." We cannot compare a parable which is common to these two Gospels, without being struck with this. For instance, in St. Matthew we read, "The kingdom of heaven is like to a certain king, which made a marriage for his son, and sent out his servants to call them that were bidden, but they would not come." In St. Luke it is, "A certain man made a great supper, and bade many; but they would not come." So in the parable of the Vineyard, which I have already shown is not one of the similitudes of the "kingdom of heaven," in St. Matthew we read, "There was a certain householder, (in the original, *oikodespotes*, a title of authority), which planted a vineyard." In St. Luke, in the same parable, we have simply, "A certain man planted a vineyard." In St. Mark too, for he shows the Servant, the title of honor is dropped: it is only "A certain man."

One other point I must not omit. Only in this Gospel is

° I may add here, as marking the exactness with which these terms are used, that, in Matt. 12:28, our Lord who had before been preaching *"the kingdom of heaven is* at hand," changes His phrase, saying, "If I by the Spirit of God cast out devils, then *the kingdom of God* is come unto you." The "kingdom of God" had *come,* because God's King was there. But for the same reason, the "kingdom of heaven" was not come, but *coming,* when the King should be cast out from earth, and received into heaven.

the "Church" named. Here in the Gospel of the Kingdom it has a very distinct mention. Rejected by Israel, "He left them and departed." Then from His disciples He receives a confession, in reply to which He names His own "Church"; adding a promise of "the keys of the kingdom of heaven," with power on earth "to loose and bind." Abraham's sons take Him for "John the Baptist, or Jeremias, or one of the prophets." They cannot echo the prophet's voice, "To us a Son is given." Only a poor remnant, to whom "not flesh and blood, but the Father hath revealed it," can say, "Thou art Christ, the Son of the living God." This is that knowledge which marks the Church; for of her it is said, that she is "to come in the knowledge of the Son of God unto a perfect man" (Eph. 4:13). At once the Lord replies, — and the words are only here, — "Thou art Peter, and upon this rock I will build my Church, and the gates of hell shall not prevail against it: and I will give thee the keys of the kingdom of heaven, and whatsoever thou shalt bind on earth shall be bound in heaven, and whatsoever thou shalt loose on earth shall be loosed in heaven": words full of import touching "the kingdom," and therefore recorded here; and for the same reason omitted in all the other Gospels.

Then comes the Transfiguration, here, and here only, introduced with words, plainly directing us to recognize that display as a glimpse or sample of the coming kingdom. After this the disciples ask, "Who is the greatest in the kingdom of heaven?" elsewhere it is simply, "They disputed who should be the greatest." The Lord replies, "Except ye be converted" — (by the way, this also is peculiar to St. Matthew, and like the word "righteousness," is strikingly characteristic of the coming kingdom) — "Except ye be converted, and become as little children, ye shall not enter the kingdom of heaven; and whosoever will humble himself as a little child, the same shall be greatest in the kingdom of heaven." Then He adds here, and here only, another word touching "the Church." "If thy brother trespass against thee, tell him his fault alone. If he will not hear thee, tell it to the Church. And if he will not hear the Church, let him be to thee as a heathen man and a publican. Verily I say unto thee, Whatsoever ye shall bind on earth shall be bound in heaven, and whatsoever ye shall loose on earth shall be loosed in heaven. For where two or three are gathered together in my name, there am I in the midst of them." All this, together with the parable immediately added in reply to the question, "How oft shall my brother trespass, and I forgive him?" is only to be found in this Gospel. The parable is a prophetic sketch of the Church's judgment for want of mercy. But on this I will not enter here. Suffice it to say that the whole passage, as it is peculiar, bears with no uncertain aim on the Lord's relation to the Church and the kingdom.

These examples — and they are but a part of the evidence which might be adduced — may suffice to show the character of this Gospel, and give the clue to those who wish to search further. I now turn for a moment to the special teaching these peculiarities contain; for not the Jew only, but the Church also, needs the lesson here.

First, then, as to the character of the kingdom, much is taught in what is distinctive here. Take the peculiarity that in St. Matthew only the Lord's kingdom is always entitled the "kingdom of heaven." Has nothing been lost by neglecting to observe that the Gospel, which reveals the kingdom, reveals it by a special name, remarkably characteristic of the position of all its true subjects? How many a mistake would have been prevented had it been seen that the true kingdom was not of earth, nor of times and places, but indeed "of heaven." Where could the claims of that system rest which makes Rome and a man there its center, if it were understood that as Rome is not heaven, so Roman Catholic has nothing akin to the "kingdom of heaven" here spoken of? Had it simply been said, "kingdom of God," the answer might of course be made, that as Israel, an earthly people with an earthly center, were once the kingdom of God, so an earthly people with an earthly center still might be that kingdom. But the Gospel which reveals the kingdom specially marks it as the "kingdom of heaven," in which neither Rome, nor time, nor earth, have any place.

But the Church has erred even as the Jew, looking for a repetition of the old thing, rather than for that new creation of righteousness and joy and peace, which is indeed the true kingdom. Nor does the fact that the prophetic parables (such as the Tares, the Leaven, and the Mustard-seed), foretell the outward results of the kingdom, as a mixed and worldly thing, prove it to be right or normal, any more than the predictions of Israel's fall prove that their rejection of Christ, which also was foretold, was agreeable to the mind of God. Out of both, God can perform His purpose; but this does not prove that the fallen and spoiled thing is that which God looks for.

Take another peculiarity. In this Gospel our Lord, as Heir of the Kingdom, is presented to us as "Son of David, Son of Abraham." This title bespeaks in mystery the character of the kingdom. In more than one Epistle, St. Paul labors to show how much is involved in this lineage. What then is taught in the words, "Son of David, Son of Abraham"; inasmuch as an heir of the kingdom must not only be Abraham's son, but Abraham's son in one special line? St. Paul thus answers: —"Neither because they are the seed of Abraham are they all children of the kingdom, but, In Isaac shall thy seed be called; that is," (this is an inspired comment), "They which are the children of the flesh, these are not the children of God, but the children of the promise are counted for the seed" (Rom. 9:7, 8). "For it is written, that Abraham had two sons, the one by a bond-maid, the other by a free-woman" (Gal. 4:22-31).

A child of the bond-maid, though Abraham's son, was not an heir of the kingdom. David and the kings all sprang from the long-barren free-woman. Which things are a mystery. The sons of the bond-maid, though Abraham's seed, were born according to nature, by human will and energy. For Hagar is the law, and her sons — children of bondage — are a figure of those who, though born in the house of the elect, and in one sense his seed, being born only by nature are not the true seed. The true heirs are of another generation, the sons of the free-woman, born when Abraham and Sarah are as good as dead; a figure of that spiritual seed which is born contrary to nature, which, like Isaac, is offered as a sacrifice, and yet lives. This is the line of the kingdom: this is the chosen seed. "He saith not, Seeds, as of many, but, To thy seed, which is Christ" (Gal. 3:16), and His body. These are heirs of the kingdom, according to the description in this Gospel, sons of Abraham, according to David's line. Let such as count themselves to be heirs see that they have this lineage; that they are sons, not by nature or fleshly energy, but by Divine power.

Take another peculiarity of this Gospel: the connection of the laws of the kingdom with the old law. The teaching on this point, as it is peculiar here, throws much light on the whole question of that on which the kingdom rests. The Lord distinctly says here, "I am not come to destroy, but to fulfil, the law." How then can we say that "we are not under the law, but under grace?" And if, as these words seem to imply, grace contrasts with law, how is it that with precepts of grace the law is yet fulfilled? Our Lord's words peculiar to this Gospel, "Thus, it becometh us to fulfil all righteousness," taken in connection with the occasion when they were uttered, may answer this question. It was at His baptism, when He presented Himself to receive that sign of death and the grave° that He spake thus of "fulfilling all righteousness."

It is when His followers take the same place, content to die that they may live, that righteousness will be seen in them also. I would it were more clearly seen that there can be no righteousness or fulfilling of the law without death; nay more, that obedient or disobedient law can only kill man. If I am perfectly obedient, the law will kill me, for it says, "Love God and man perfectly"; and such a love would soon consume me. If I am disobedient, it will kill me, for it is written, "Cursed is every one that contin-

---

° "We are buried by baptism" ROM. 6:4.

ueth not in all things that are written in the book of the law
to do them": clearly proving that the law was not given to
save us, but, as St. Paul teaches, to be a standard to show us
that we are ruined sinners. A law which could have given
life could not be given to fallen man. Hence the Scripture by
the law only concludes all men under sin. Grace comes in,
thanks be to God; but it meets man in death. He must confess himself dead, (therefore we are baptized), and die,
too, if the law is ever to be fulfilled in him. And no sooner
do we take the place of dead ones, and own our lot as sons
of men, than heaven and the kingdom of heaven is at once
opened to us. Then this grace produces grace. Christ died
for us, and we ought to lay down our lives for the brethren.
And then, if dying be the fulfilling of the law, we need not
strive for life here, we need not take "eye for eye," or "hate
our enemies." We may be content to suffer and die, and
act in grace to all, knowing that, if we lose all, the kingdom
of heaven is yet ours.

Will the law be broken thus, because we are "not under,"
but above it? Nay, thus only will it be fulfilled. I venture
to say that till men are content to die, — till they see that
"fulfilling all righteousness" is connected with our taking
the place of dead and buried sinners, — the precepts of the
Sermon on the Mount will never be kept, however much
they may be lauded by us. Take that law, hoping to live
by it, and it must be pared down. Take it to die by, as part
of the story of the cross, and it is all clear.

Another peculiarity of this Gospel is the special light
which it throws upon the position of the true heirs of the
kingdom, as respects their carnal brethren. Are the true
heirs, like Pharisees, to separate themselves from those in
error, and to thank God that they are not as other men; or
shall they go out with a few, like Theudas (Acts 5:36, 37),
into the wilderness, in the hope of again finding the original
circumstances of the dispensation?

The true Heir, with a heart of love, takes neither course.
He will not stand alone, but will take His place among the
lost ones. And He took it though the religious people

judged Him for it; not like Theudas and Judas looking for Jordan to dry up, but Himself going down into its waters, and being buried under them; not fighting to re-establish the kingdom upon earth, but trusting God to lift Him out of it into a higher, even a heavenly one. And so "heaven opened" to Him, and God said, "I am well pleased." Men might be displeased, but God was "well pleased." Then, having been a brief season in the wilderness — just as opened heavens yet drive men thither for a season — He returns in the power of the world to come, to tell others how near that same heaven is to them also.

And to this day the same thing takes place in every heir of the kingdom who has reached this stage. For all have not reached it. For we may be, like Christ, heirs of the kingdom, and yet in Egypt. We may be heirs, and yet, like Him, be arguing with doctors at Jerusalem. He did so when He was twelve years old; and when He is twelve years old in us, we may do so. But if we grow with Him till with Him we see Israel's state, and then so yield to Him, that He lives and walks in us, that "to us to live is Christ," then, inasmuch as He cannot change, but is "Jesus Christ, the same yesterday, today, and forever," what He did of old, He will do again in us — go down again amongst publicans — then have heaven opened — and then, having overcome the devil, come forth to tell to others how near that kingdom is; and that the way to enter it is not by this or that outward separation, much less by boastings as to Israel's works or temple, but by repentance, by admitting our state, and by taking the place which befits a fallen people: expecting there to find our God and His grace sufficient for us.

Many other points might be adduced, growing out of what is special here: but with one other particular I must conclude. We noticed in this Gospel a special allusion to the Prophets. The expression, "Then was fulfilled that which was spoken by the prophet," is peculiar to this Gospel. And yet the children of the kingdom knew not the Heir when He appeared. Though fulfilling their own Scriptures before them, He was a wonder to them. People in darkness saw light. He neither strove nor cried. The broken reed was not bruised, nor the smoking flax quenched. But so low was Israel fallen, that they knew not the day of their visitation. Like looked for like, and so they esteemed Him not.

Had He come, like Barabbas, to strive for the restoration of the earthly kingdom, or had He sought to overthrow the existing rule of Herod, He should not have stood alone. But because His kingdom, is heavenly, Israel cared not for it. He may go whither He will: they want Him not. Such has been, such must be, the experience of the true heirs. They may in their lives fulfil the prophets, manifesting light, and grace, and righteousness. But if they will not fight for or against the outward things of their day by other outward things, the children of the kingdom, born after the flesh, either cannot discern, or will not have them. Let the heirs be prepared for their lot, to be rejected even by Abraham's sons; for of Abraham's sons it is written, "They which are born after the flesh persecute those which are born after the Spirit." But the mocked ones have their reward. If the kingdom of earth is closed, the "kingdom of heaven" is open to them.

In that day when the King now hidden shall be revealed to men, may we, now content to be hidden with Him, be partakers of His glory. They that suffer in the mystery of the kingdom shall rejoice in its revelation. Till that revelation, may we be in "the kingdom and patience of Jesus Christ." *Amen.*

Mark's View

"The second living creature was like unto a Calf" Rev. 4:7.
"Much increase is by the strength of the Ox" Prov. 14:4.

"THE SECOND LIVING CREATURE was like unto an Ox." And the second Gospel reveals the Lord in that aspect of which the Ox is the appointed figure. He stands here as the patient Servant and Sacrifice for others, spending and being spent to serve the sons of men. The first glance at this Gospel does not give us the same broad distinction which meets us upon the very face of the other three. A second look will prove that it has marks, which are in their way quite as conclusive and characteristic as the unmistakeable distinctions of the other Gospels.* And though the peculiarities are, I own, minute, yet this is compensated for the fact that they are very many, and meet us again and again in every page. The strokes may be faint, and the touches fine, but their very fineness shows a Master's hand, which without the exaggeration of caricature, by lines too minute to arrest the careless eye, can present a perfect picture. Of course, the subject itself in the main is the same in all the Gospels; the Lord's life being the material of each narrative; but this only makes the distinctions more instructive: and though the disputer of this world may stumble, the humble imitator of God is richly taught.

I now proceed to these distinctions, which I may arrange

---

* The fact that one sect of early heretics chose this Gospel in preference to the others, on account of its contents, proves that at that day something distinctive could be seen in it.

as, first, the omissions, secondly, the additions, peculiar to this Gospel. From both we shall be able to note what is special and characteristic in the view of Christ here presented to us.

And here before I notice the omissions, I would observe how much may be gathered, not only from what is taught, but also from what is omitted, in certain parts of Holy Scripture. Even had no Apostle shown us the signifcance of a slight omission, one with right thoughts of God might have anticipated that the whole form of a revelation from Him, and thus its omissions, could not be without reason. But, as ever, in pity to the ignorant and weak, the Lord gives us an example to show what we may expect in, and how we ought to read, His Word. Thus writing to the Hebrews, the Apostle points out how much is to be learned from the simple fact, that in the history of Melchizedek, nothing is narrated either of his birth or death. He is presented to us "without father, or mother, without descent or pedigree, having neither beginning of days nor end of life" (Heb. 7:3). And this omission, says the Apostle, is with purpose, and full of teaching, specially intended to show how One should arise, both king and priest, who in the fullest sense should be "without beginning of days, or end of life."

Equally instructive, as many know, are the omissions in other types, and to take a broader example, the omissions in the Books of Chronicles as compared with the history given in the Books of Kings. An apprehension of God's purpose in each of these books shows how significant the omission is, and how, in ways the world cannot see, God's wisdom is revealed to His own, even if they be babes and sucklings. It is the same in the case of the Gospels. Be it omission or addition, each is perfect; and for the eye that can see it, (though, indeed, few are seers — "a seer is a prophet"), both are equally subjects for instructive contemplation.

As to the omissions then in this Gospel, many points might be adduced. I confine myself to the more obvious

ones, which I would now note in order. Here, then, is no
genealogy, no miraculous birth, no reference to Bethlehem,
or adoration of the wise men, as in St. Matthew's Gospel.
No childhood at Nazareth, no subjection to His parents, no
increase in wisdom and stature, as in St. Luke; no reference to His pre-existence and Divine glory, as in St. John's
Gospel. All these points, important in their bearing on the
kingdom or person of the Lord, would be out of place in
the description of His service, and therefore have no place
here.

On the contrary, St. Mark comes at once to service, touching for a moment on that of the Baptist, quoting his testimony that One should follow who should baptize not with
water only but with the Holy Spirit; and then passing di-
rectly, without further preface to the Lord's own ministry,
in exact accordance with his opening words, "The beginning
of the Gospel of Jesus Christ, the Son of God." The service
here is such service as can only be rendered by one who
rejoices that He is indeed a Son of God; by one who fully
understands that not by service are we made sons, but by
sonship may we become servants. When, therefore, St.
Mark tells us that this is "the Gospel of the Son," we are
prepared for service springing from the assurance of sonship — evangelical service as opposed to legal. It is this
"Gospel," this ministry or service, which St. Mark is about
to draw; and, omitting what does not bear on this, he
comes straight to the details of this ministry.

Then here is no Sermon on the Mount. The laws of the
kingdom would be out of place, for the Servant, not the
King, is here manifested. Here is no "Our Father," which,
so full of character in St. Matthew and St. Luke, as illustrating the wants and relationships both of the Jew and
Gentile, is here omitted as having no special bearing on the
path of service. For the same reason we have here no
lengthy discourses, and but few parables; for the service
here is rather doing than teaching. There are both, but the
mind of the Spirit seems to be occupied more with the

former of these than with the latter. Doing, and toiling, and serving the needy is far humbler work than teaching.

As teacher one holds more of a place of authority than is consistent with the idea of pure service. Here the service presented is that of which the Ox is the fittest emblem, a service of which very little in spite of abounding preaching is to be discovered now. In a word, throughout this Gospel, as another has said, it is not Christ's claim on men, so much as man's claim on Christ, and His grace and power, which the Spirit here witnesses. Thus, while authoritative discourses and parables are few compared with the corresponding chapters of the other Gospels, the details of service are given far more minutely.

And yet, though for the most part parables are omitted, there is one peculiar to this Gospel, in which, as we might anticipate from the fact of its insertion only here, we have something characteristic and instructive as to true ministry. Indeed, I believe that all the parables given in this Gospel — there are but four* — bear upon this question. But as to that parable which is only here, of "the Seed which grew secretly, first the blade, then the ear, and then the full corn," what is it but an encouragement to servants to sow in faith, and then leave results to Him who only can give increase?

It seems to me as if the Lord himself here spoke out of the abundance of His heart; that He was expressing His own assurance of a full return for all His sore travail; and that in prospect of His death He rejoiced in the thought that whether the sower "sleep or rise," the seed should yet spring up and increase greatly. I find in St. Matthew in the corresponding place, that instead of this parable, which here comes in between that of "the Sower," and "the Mustard-seed"; there, between these same parables, we have that of "the Tares," which finds no place in this Gospel. The

---

* The Sower, the Seed which grew secretly, the Mustard-seed, (ch. 4) and the Wicked Husbandmen, (ch. 12). The connection of the truth contained in each of these four parables with ministry is obvious.

reason is plain. The parable of "the Tares" gives our Lord
the place of power. Such words as these, "In the time of
harvest, I will say to the reapers, Gather first the tares, and
bind them in bundles, and burn them," though exactly
suited to the Lord of the kingdom, are for that very reason
out of character here, and as such are not recorded.

To continue the notice of omissions. Here is no arraign-
ment of the nation, no sentence passed upon Jerusalem as
in the other Gospels. I look in vain for the repeated judgment, "Woe unto you," so marked in St. Matthew; but instead of this, in the corresponding chapter, Jesus is here
represented as sitting opposite to the treasury, and watching a poor widow.* If the Lord must judge, the Servant has
an eye for service: unsparingly spending His own life for
men, He can see and appreciate the spending of the last
farthing. Here as everywhere the thing noticed answers to
the beholder's state. Oh, that this fact, so continually meeting us in these Gospels, might awaken some by what they
see to discover where and what they are!

Again, in the prophecy on the Mount of Olives, here is
no Bridegroom, as in St. Matthew, receiving the wise and
rejecting the foolish virgins; here is no Lord judging between faithful and unfaithful servants; no King, enthroned
in glory, separating the nations to the right and left hand.
But on the contrary, here only we read, touching the coming of the Son of Man, "Of that day, and that hour, knoweth no man, no, not the angels which are in heaven, neither
the Son, but the Father" (Chap. 13:32), — words which,
as they are peculiar to this Gospel, so also are very characteristic: for here the Son is seen with glory laid aside,
clothed in the likeness of man, in very deed a true Servant.

And in this aspect, like other servants, He awaits another's
will, not knowing the lord's secrets; for "the servant knoweth not what his lord doeth" (John 15:15). And so as
Servant He says, naming Himself with other blessed servants, the holy angels — "Of that day knoweth no man, no,

---

* Compare Matt. 21-23 with Mark 12.

not the angels, neither the Son, but the Father." Nor does this touch the truth of His Person; for that is not the question here. But just as in St. Luke the words, "He increased in wisdom and stature, and in favor with God and man," speak of Him as Son of Adam, without in any way contradicting that He is also "the Word made flesh"; just as His death in one aspect is spoken of as "a sweet savor," man freely giving to God what is most sweet to Him, while in another aspect it is regarded as penal and a sin-offering, the due judgment for the sins of men; so in like manner what is true of Him as Servant does not deny His lordship, which is but another view of the same wondrous and blessed Lord.

And these omissions continue to the end. Thus in the Garden, here is no reference to His right to summon twelve legions of angels had He so willed it. Here is no promise of the kingdom on the cross to His dying companion; here is no notice of the resurrection and appearance of saints, accompanying the Lord, as freed by Him, when He arose and led captivity captive. Such acts or claims, perfect in St. Matthew, are out of the purpose of the Spirit here, and as such find no place in this Gospel. So in the last scene, the commission to the Apostles to go and preach, the points here recorded, when compared with what St. Matthew gives us, are very striking.* There, as befits the Lord of the kingdom, we read that He came and said, "All power is given to me in heaven and in earth: go ye therefore, and make disciples of all nations, teaching them to observe all things whatsoever I have commanded you." Surely the Lord of the kingdom comes out in every word.

In St. Mark this is omitted, but we have, "Go ye into all the world, preach the gospel to every creature: he that believeth and is baptized shall be saved, and he that believeth not shall be damned." For here He is not discipling as with authority, or commanding that "all things which He has commanded should be observed in all nations"; but rather,

---

* Matt. 28:18-20, and Mark 16:15-20.

as knowing the path of service, He hints at the rejection as well as the success, which His servants will surely meet with. "He that believeth, and he that believeth not" — what a tale is in the words; how do they express the experience of One who knows all the results even of the best service! Now His disciples are to take His place, and He will serve in them: even yet shall His work be accomplished in His members; and so in this Gospel only we have the special promise of power through His name, to work even as He worked (Chap. 16:17, 18). Then the Gospel thus closes, "They went forth and preached, *the Lord working* with them, and confirming the word with signs following"; for He is yet the Worker, though risen. So wonderfully, to the very end, does this Gospel preserve its own distinct character; from its opening words, beginning with "the Gospel of Jesus Christ," down to the promise of the spread of it through His servants to all nations.

I have thus marked some of the chief omissions which strike us in St. Mark; but, even in what is recorded, and where in substance the narrative follows St. Matthew, there is in this Gospel ever a lower and softened tone. Thus in John's testimony to Jesus, this Evangelist stops short, omitting the prediction, that "He should burn the chaff with fire unquenchable." So in the account of the ordination of "the twelve," in St. Matthew we read that "He sent them forth, and commanded them saying, Go not thus, but go thus and thus," as with authority. In St. Mark we read, "He ordained twelve that they might be with Him"; they are regarded rather as His companions in service, in which relation they are seen throughout this whole Gospel.

For — and it is very characteristic — never do they call Him "Lord" in this Gospel. On the contrary, the word is remarkably omitted, till after His resurrection, in scenes where it occurs in the corresponding place in the other Gospels. For example, when the leper comes, in St. Matthew he says, "Lord, if thou wilt, thou canst make me

---

* Compare Mark 1:8, and Matt. 3:11, 12.

clean." In St. Mark I read, "A leper came beseeching Him, and saying, If thou wilt, thou canst make me clean." So at the supper. In St. Matthew, "They began to say, Lord, is it I?" In St. Mark, "They began to say unto Him, one by one, Is it I? and another said, Is it I?" The word "Lord" is markedly omitted. So in the case of the dumb child, the father cries out, "Lord, I believe; help thou mine unbelief." In our authorised version I find "Lord" inserted here in St. Mark; but Griesbach, without the slightest reference to the character of the Gospel, marks this word as one which is "absolutely spurious," and which as such has no place in his version. So in the storm. In St. Matthew we read that the disciples cried, "Lord, save us." We look in vain for such a word in the corresponding place in St. Mark's Gospel.

Is this chance? Surely, if not a sparrow falls to the ground without being marked, a title of the beloved Son is not dropped out of a Gospel without the Father's knowledge. The omission or change here is of a piece with the form of His ancient Word, now speaking of Elohim, now of Shaddai, now of Jehovah, suiting His titles according to the matter in hand, and His own relation to it, as Creator, Protector, or God in covenant.* The taught of the Father know this, and rejoice to trace His wisdom, even where

---

* Those acquainted with the Old Testament know that the name of God varies according to the subject-matter. Thus in Genesis 1 God is Elohim. In Gen. 2 He is Jehovah-Elohim. A title suffices to describe Him in the work of creation, which is not enough when His relation to His creature man comes to be described. In a deeper sense I may say, God is known by a different name in the days of labor, and in that Paradise whether man is set in relationship to God as lord of all. In Psalm 91:1, we have four titles of the Lord brought into the compass of a single sentence. "He that dwelleth in the secret place of the *Most High,* (the name by which He was known to Melchizedek, 'priest of the Most High God,') shall abide under the shadow of the *Almighty,* (the name by which He was known to Abraham;) I will say of *Jehovah,* (the covenant name for Israel,) He is my refuge and my fortress; my *God,* (my Elohim,) in Him will I trust." To the believer the names of God are full of meaning, as revelations of His nature, and property, and covenant-relationships.

others, making their blindness the judge of all things, can perceive no beauty.

But it is time I should turn from omissions to what is positively distinctive here. And though I am sure that only one well practised in showing kindness can see the whole of these wonders, though a servant's eye may be needed to know the import of some touches here, the heart must be hard indeed, which sees nothing in the details peculiar to this Gospel. Trifling as each is by itself, the aggregate of the whole is an amount of teaching, from which the best-trained servant may continually draw some fresh lesson.

The first point I notice then is the fact, here only recorded, in the temptation, that "He was with the wild beasts." This is a true mark of him who can serve, that, like David of old, he has, in the wilderness and alone, overcome the lion and the bear before in public he fights against Goliath. Let such as would serve lay this to heart. If called to service, they may expect for a season to be among the wild beasts. Alone with God, let us overcome such. Then we may go forth and fight for, and serve, Israel.

The next thing I observe is the remarkable repetition of the word, "forthwith." We cannot read a single chapter carefully, or consult a Concordance — of course a Greek Concordance should be used, for the same word, *eutheos,* is in our version indifferently translated, "straightway," "forthwith," and "immediately" — without being struck with the recurrence of this word. Thus, to take but a single chapter — the first may serve as an example — Jesus is baptized, and then *"immediately"* He is driven into the wilderness. Then when He returns and begins His service, "He saw James and John, and *straightway* He called them, and they went after Him. And they went into Capernaum, and *straightway* on the Sabbath-day He entered into a synagogue, and taught, and cast out an unclean spirit. . . . And *forthwith,* when they came out of the synagogue, they entered into Simon's house; and Simon's wife's mother was sick, and *anon* (the same word) they tell Him of her. . . .

And there came a leper, and as soon as He had spoken *immediately* the leprosy departed . . . and *forthwith* He sent him away. And again He entered into Capernaum, and *straightway* many were gathered . . . and *immediately,* when Jesus perceived that they reasoned in their hearts, He said," etc. Now this runs through the Gospel, and is peculiar to it;* and when it is taken in connection with other expressions, such as "in the way," "in the house," "as He sat at meat," or "as He walked in the temple," we get a glimpse of what is meant by "instant in season, out of season," and what befits one who is called to be the Lord's servant.

Then as to the way in which He served. We have here many details, as to His demeanor, and bearing, and looks, not to be found in any other Gospel. Thus in the case of the little children who were brought that He should touch them, here only do we read, that "He *took them up in His arms,* and blessed them." So again, of the child whom He set in the midst, here only, "He *took him in His arms."* Here only is it seen of Peter's wife's mother, that "He *took her by the hand and lifted her up."* So again, here only do we read, "He *took the blind man by the hand."* Here only is it noticed of the child which had the dumb spirit, that "Jesus *took him by the hand and lifted him up."*

I need not stop to speak of the tenderness these acts display; but I believe many have yet to learn what ought to be, and has been, the effect of the touch and hand of God's servants. I know that "laying on of hands" is now by many regarded as a mere form. I will only say, the time was when virtue accompanied the hand of God's servants; indeed, when even the shadow of an Apostle could heal. It will not hurt us to remember, even if the glory is now departed from us, that such things have once been. And this I will add, that should the day return when devils are rebuked,

---

* I see, by a reference to Schmid's Concordance, that the word *eutheos* occurs only eighty times in the New Testament, and of these instances forty are found in the short Gospel of St. Mark.

and lame ones healed, those who look closely will see that a tender hand will not be wanting in such service. "But where," as one has asked, "are the layers on of hands, who give man to himself and God, by casting out his devils? Where is the clergy to whom sickness makes its last appeal for health? We find them among the fishermen of the first century, but not among our pastors now. Many say that the age of miracle is past and gone. But Christianity, as we find it in Scripture, was the institution of miracle. And if the age of miracle is well-nigh gone, it it not because the age of Christianity is well-nigh gone? The age of mathematics would be past, if no man cultivated them." But here I forbear. Let us be content to take beggars by the hand: we may then see things wholly out of the range of our present field of vision.

Again in this Gospel the look is noticed, and this in scenes where the other Evangelists in the corresponding places give us no such information. Thus, when they watched Him upon the Sabbath, whether He would heal or not, we read here, "*When he had looked round about on them in anger*" — was there nothing in such a look? So again, when they said, "Thy mother and Thy brethren without seek for Thee"; here only is it noticed, that "*He looked round about* on them who sat about Him, and said, Behold my mother and my brethren." So again, when He spoke of His cross, and Peter began to rebuke Him, here only we read, "And when He turned about, *and looked on* His disciples, He rebuked Peter." There must have been something in that look never to be forgotten; a flash of light, a beam of the glory, which made its dwelling in that lowly Servant.

So again, in the case of him who came kneeling down and asking, "What shall I do to inherit eternal life?" here only do we read, that "Jesus *looking upon him*, loved him"; and then again, "when he went away grieved," here only it is noticed, that "Jesus *looking round* said to His disciples, How hardly shall they that have riches enter into the kingdom of God!" Surely not in vain is the look recorded. Let

servants mark this: there is no small ministry in a single
look, be it of love, or grief, or anger. It may speak what
words cannot express. It has ere now, in storm and calm,
mid the rush of battle, and in scenes of deep anguish, im-
parted confidence and peace beyond the power of language. For it speaks truly: hence its deep power. And
indeed heaven may be in an eye, its sunshine and rain; and
if it be there, though there be no speech nor language, its
voice shall still be heard. Oh, for a look like that of the
Master! Oh, for that light of life within, breaking forth
through eyes beaming with love and holiness!

To do justice to my subject is beyond me, but as I have
spoken of the acts and looks, I may add a reference or two
to some of those words of ministry which are peculiar to
this Gospel. One example we find in the raising of the
daughter of Jairus. The scene is common to three Evangelists, but here only do we get some particulars full of
marked tenderness. Thus St. Mark alone relates, that when
some said, Thy daughter is dead, "Jesus, *as soon as He
heard the word that was spoken*," (as if to save the father
a moment's anguish and unbelief), "*said, Be not afraid*";
brief words, but full of grace, revealing the Servant's heart,
who, even while He healed, watched to aid the spiritual
progress of those He came to comfort.

In the same spirit of mindful affection is Peter specially
named here, when after the resurrection a message is sent
by the women to the disciples. In St. Matthew the angels
say, "Go and tell His disciples": here only, "Tell His disciples, *and Peter*, that He goeth before you into Galilee."
For, more than the rest, Peter needed a special word, and
so above the rest he is remembered. The good Shepherd,
who loves all, has peculiar pity towards the wounded sheep.
Thus did this Servant of servants speak a word in season:
"He spake," as St. Mark tells us, (and the words are peculiar to this Gospel), "as they were able to bear it" (Chap.
4:33); with milk for babes, and meat for the strong, distrib-
uting His words, even as His acts, in special pity to the
feeble, showing more abundant grace to that which lacked.

Another point peculiar to this Gospel is the repeated notice we get here of the way in which our Lord permitted Himself to be intruded upon in His retirement, and indeed upon all occasions. So thoroughly was He at the disposal of others (here only is it noticed) that "He could not so much as eat"; for the multitude came together, and it was not in the heart of that blessed Servant to refuse Himself to their importunities.

This occurs again and again. Thus after a day of toil, the Lord, rising up early, "went and departed into a solitary place, and there prayed: but Simon and they that were with him, followed after Him; and when they found Him, they said unto Him, All men seek for Thee." Without a murmur He at once receives them, allowing the interruption, and says, "Let us go into the next towns, and preach there also, for therefore am I sent" (Chap. 1:35-38). We find nothing answering to this in the other Gospels. So again, when His apostles returned from their mission, and gathered themselves together to Him, Jesus says, (and the words are only here), "Come ye yourselves apart into a desert place, and rest awhile"; thus showing not only His tender sympathy for them, but teaching how needful retirement is for those who serve others. "So they departed into a desert place by ship privately." But scarce had they got there before "the people ran afoot thither, and came together to Him."

Jesus at once allows the intrusion. He had sought to be alone, nevertheless He rises, and teaches them; and then, because it was a desert place, and they were faint, He feeds them, making His own ease give place to their need. And then, O perfect service! remembering His weary apostles, He constrains them to get into a ship and go away to the other side, "while He sent away the people"(Chap. 6: 31-45). So again, at the close of a day, "when even was come," wearied with toil, He enters a ship with His disciples to pass over to the other side. We read, "They took Him even as He was" (Chap. 4:36), — a remarkable expression, peculiar to this Gospel, and descriptive of His extreme weariness. No sooner is He in the ship than He is asleep. But a storm alarms the disciples; they break in upon His rest; and (in this Gospel only are His words on this occasion given) without a murmur He arises to calm their troubled spirits. Oh, how different from us! Our times of rest must be our own. Sleeping or waking, He lives for others. If others need Him, He is their Servant, "always girded," ever ready to do them good.

And here I may notice that this Evangelist records two miracles, which, as they are peculiar to this Gospel, are also very characteristic of what befits true ministry. The one is the case of "him who was deaf" (Chap. 7:32-37); the other, of the blind man at Bethsaida (Chap. 8:22-26). In both I find not only in word, but in act, the Lord manifesting a desire to throw a veil of secrecy over these gracious actions. And surely this is one unfailing mark of service according to God, "alms in secret," "the right hand ignorant of what the left hand doeth." This comes out brightly here. We read, "He *took him aside,* and charged them that they should tell no man": again, "He took the blind man by the hand, *and led him out of the town,* and said, Neither go into the town, nor tell it to any in the town." Words like these requiring secrecy, though not so frequently repeated, may be found elsewhere: but acts in which the Servant so remarkably strives to hide Himself, are peculiar to this Gospel. So in the case of the woman of Canaan, here only it is added, "He entered into a house, and *would have no man know it.*" For this is perfection in service, — to serve unseen, unthanked.

Such service is heavenly, like that of the holy angels. "Are they not all ministering spirits?" and yet who sees them, who thanks them? Nor do they ask, nor would they receive, our praise. Enough for them that they are doing the will of God; for they know, that "in keeping, as well as for keeping, His commandments is great reward." Surely not in vain are ministers addressed as "angels of churches" (Rev. 2:1ff.). May such as count themselves to hold this place, see that tried by this test of unseen service they walk worthy of it.

The peculiarities hitherto noticed refer to what was open in the Lord's service. But several deep and precious secrets of ministry are told out in the peculiarities of this Gospel, as God alone can tell them. Take, for instance, the secret of power. Do any ask, how is it gained? We read here that after having spent a day, healing the hearts and sicknesses of all about him — in this one day alone we read that He taught in the synagogue, cast out a devil, healed Peter's wife's mother, and at even relieved the many who were gathered about the door — after such a day it is added, "*And in the morning rising up a great while before day*, He went out to a solitary place, and there prayed" (Chap. 1:35); words which, as they are peculiar to this Gospel, speak with no uncertain voice the one prime secret of all real power in true ministry.

Another secret comes out in those references to the exercises of our Lord's soul, which are quite peculiar to this Gospel. Thus, here only do we read, when the leper came, that "Jesus *was moved with compassion*." The act of healing is mentioned in St. Matthew and St. Luke; but St. Mark alone gives a glimpse of the exercise of heart in our Lord which accompanied the outward service. So in the feeding of the multitude, here again the heart is laid bare: we read that "When He came out, and saw much people, *He was moved with compassion toward them*, and began to teach them many things." So again, when the young ruler comes — a scene common to the other Gospels — here only is it recorded that "Jesus beholding him, *loved him*." This excercise of soul, the secret of all service, comes out in this Gospel, and only here. As a key to service, here it is quite perfect, teaching a lesson many need to learn, that without love the most costly service will be unlike the Lord's, and all barren.

Another secret of service is noticed in the cure of the child possessed with an unclean spirit. The scene generally is common to two of the other Gospels; but here only do we read that the father of the child cried out, *"If thou canst do anything*, have compassion on us," to which the Lord instantly replies, in words only found in this Gospel, *"If thou canst believe, all things are possible"* (Chap. 9:22). A deep secret of ministry is here. Not only must love be in the servant, but there must be faith on the part of the patient who comes to seek the blessing. I can only serve those who trust me. And agreeable to this we read again — words only to be found in this Gospel — that in a certain place *"He could do no mighty works, because of their unbelief"* (Chap. 6:5, 6); showing how the most loving service is of no avail if met by unbelief, while faith draws yet more of the riches of God's hidden treasures out of His servants' hands.

One other point, and I have done. In no Evangelist but St. Mark do I find the same detail as to the special trials, inward and outward, which our Lord suffered. I say nothing of His weary days, that "He had no leisure so much as to eat" — a circumstance twice recorded in this Gospel, and only here: but His *"grief for their hardness of heart"* (Chap. 3:5), an expression peculiar to this Gospel, lifts the veil, and shows something of the wear of spirit which His service cost this blessed Servant. So again, here only do we find the reproach — "They said, He is beside Himself" (Chap. 3:21) — because His service lacked that selfish prudence which a selfish world praises; a reproach which an Apostle felt so keenly that he answers it, saying, "If we be beside ourselves, or sober, it is for your sake"; a reproach felt by our Lord, but unanswered, save by the answer of a yet ceaseless, unmurmuring, patient, loving service.

Then in this Gospel only do we read, that "He *marvelled* because of their unbelief," when they refer to His calling, in answer to His works, saying, "Is not this the Carpenter?" Here only do we read that "He *sighed*," and again, that "He *sighed deeply*"; for in His service He did not offer to God that which cost Him nothing; teaching us too that if we would serve as He did, there must be many "sighs," the fruit first of sympathy with the pain around us, and then of rejected kindnesses. Then again, here only are we told, when He was led out to suffer, that "*They bear Him.*" First we read, "*They led Him* out that they might crucify Him": but He seems to have failed under the burden, for soon "They compel another to bear His cross"; and then St. Mark tells us "*They bear* Him," as if actually supporting Him, "to the place called Golgotha." A fit end to such unsparing labor. He was worn out, and needed to be borne, and long before the thieves crucified with Him were dead, He had resigned His spirit. For indeed service is sacrifice throughout, and "the ox strong to labor" is also the chosen victim for the Lord's altar.

Such are some of the details peculiar to this Gospel, and very plainly do they show that true ministry is no slight "warfare"; that service, "according to the pattern seen on the mount," is something very different from the correct drawing-room Christianity of the present day. And this deep sense of the cross, as the price of service, comes out all through this Gospel. A single word added to what is recorded by the other Evangelists, again and again sets this in the very clearest light. Thus, when the young man comes and asks, "What lack I yet?" in St. Matthew the Lord's answer is, "Sell that thou hast, and give to the poor, and thou shalt have treasure in heaven." St. Mark, in recording the same scene, repeats these words, only adding, "*And take up thy cross*"; for the Servant, though He has made Himself poor, does not the less feel that herein there is a cross to carry. So again, in the answer of our Lord, when "Peter began to say, Lo, we have left all, and have followed Thee," in St. Mark alone do we read that with the reward shall come the cross: — "He shall receive a hundred-fold in this time, . . . *with persecutions.*"

But enough. Blessed be God that such service has been seen on earth; that there has been such a hand, such an eye, and such a heart here, among the sons of men. And blessed be God, that by the same Spirit He waits to mold us to His pattern, yea, that He has predestinated us to be conformed to the image of His beloved Son. And if the Head was con-

tent to serve thus if, while He tarried here, He lived to
meet the need of all who sought succor; if, now risen,
He is yet the same, still the loving Worker, interceding
within the veil, and working here too for us; if He shall yet
serve us, "for the less is blessed of the greater," when in the
coming kingdom He shall still lead His flock to living foun-
tains, and wipe away their tears — shall not we whom He
has purchased, in whom He seeks to dwell, who are His
witnesses in a world which knows Him not, wait upon Him
until His mantle fall on us, and His Spirit, "the oil which
was upon the Head," run down even to us also; till we
catch the mind of heaven, and are made like unto the
angels, children of God and children of resurrection, called
to stand in the presence of God, and yet to serve, as ministering spirits to them who shall be heirs of salvation? God
is serving, — "the Father worketh."

Oh! what works of love, from the rain and fruitful seasons
up to the mighty work of raising man from earth to highest
heaven; and Christ has served, and is serving; and the
Holy Spirit is serving, taking of the things of Christ, to reveal them to us, and then to work them in us; and angels
are serving, and saints are serving, and the Church pro-
claims her call, that she too because redeemed must be a
servant here, and that her rulers are but servants, yea, servant of servants; and heaven is serving earth, and earth the
creatures on it. So let us, after our Pattern, being redeemed,
go forth to serve also. "Blessed are those servants whom
the Lord when He cometh shall find so doing. Verily, He
shall gird Himself, and make them sit down to meat, and
He will come forth and serve them."

PRAYER

O Lord, Thou canst perform it; perform it to Thy praise;
Oh! show us the glory of Thy service, full of grace and
truth, that in its presence we may be changed; and as we
have borne the image of the earthy, may even here bear
to Thy glory the image of the heavenly. *Amen.*

Luke's View

"The third living creature had a face as a Man" REV. 4:7.
"I drew them with the cords of a Man" HOS. 11:4.

"THE THIRD LIVING CREATURE had a face as a Man," agreeable to which the third Gospel sets forth the Lord as Son of Adam, or Son of Man. Unlike St. Mark, where the peculiar view of our Lord had to be gathered from nice details, each in itself comparatively trifling, yet when summed up affording a picture full of character and distinctness, St. Luke throughout writes very broadly and plainly the memoir of the Son of Man, showing the Lord as very Man, and therefore linked not only to a certain kingdom, but to all the Sons of Adam. Here is man according to God, the pattern Man, in and through whom man is blessed and God glorified, seen not only in moral perfectness, but in all the sufferings and honors, which according to God's purpose are the heritage of the sons of men; first humbled into the dust of death, then exalted to God's right hand, His image and likeness, to rule as Lord of all. For man had been God's image, set by Him to rule the creature; and though this image had failed in the first Adam, it was to be renewed with greater blessings in "the Second Man, the Lord from heaven."

This is the picture drawn by St. Luke. And as in St. Matthew, the Gospel of the Kingdom, we had the professing children of the kingdom, and their zeal for God, though not according to knowledge — their washings of the outside of the cup, their tithing mint and cummin, their compassing sea and land to make one proselyte — set very bright-

71

ly in contrast with the true Heir, and His kingdom of right-eousness, and joy, and peace, in the Holy Spirit; so here in the Gospel of the Son of Man, as the pattern Man walks before us, we have men as they are set side by side, in strong and marked contrast, with man as he should be, the Man Christ Jesus.

In this relation as Son of Man, the Lord holds two offices,* both of which, as they result from His being very Man, meet us very prominently throughout this Gospel. As Man He is the Priest, "for every high-priest is taken from among men," for this reason, "that he may have compassion on the ignorant, for that he himself also is compassed with infirmity." As Man He is the Prophet, or Apostle, sent from God, and yet feeling with those to whom He comes as God's messenger. The writer of the Epistle to the Hebrews therefore, when speaking to them, of their "Apostle and High-priest," the One who comes from God, and goes to God, for us, introduces his subject with a proof that He who holds this place is Man, showing, that "forasmuch as the children were partakers of flesh and blood, He also Himself likewise took part of the same." "For in all things it behooved Him to be made like unto His brethren, that He might be a merciful and faithful High-priest, to make reconciliation for the sins of the people. For in that He himself hath suffered being tempted, He is able to succor them that are tempted." This explains the reason why some, seeing so much of priestly compassion here, have connected this Gospel with the emblem of "the ox," taking that figure as representative of sacrifice, and so of Priest here, I cannot doubt. For the Priest is a relation, not arbitrarily undertaken, but necessarily growing out of our Lord's true manhood. But this only confirms me in this

---

* I have said that our Lord as Man holds *two* offices, because these two, Apostle, and High-priest, God's messenger to man, and man's to God, involve or are connected, I believe, with all the others, which He holds as Son of Man.

view, which indeed is justified by this Gospel throughout, that here the Lord stands before us as the "Son of Man."

To pretend to give more than a few hints would lead me too far. I shall be content here to show, how what is distinctive in St. Luke points out the Son of Man; adding two or three examples as to the way in which the peculiarities of this Gospel mark our special duties and privileges as sons of men.

Now as to what is distinctive in St. Luke. His very Preface is characteristic: here only the Evangelist begins with an address to his friend Theophilus. Human affection is thus displayed here. A Man is to be described, and the Writer will draw his friend to the subject "by the bands of a man." Then this Evangelist — and this one alone — refers to his own personal knowledge of his subject, "having had perfect understanding of all things from the very first"; thus bringing something human into his task, which this Gospel presents to us. As another has observed, "the writer himself appears, as having the faculties and affections of a man exercised about the things which were engaging him." Nor were his heart and pen the less for this reason under the guidance of the Holy Spirit, who, as He was about to draw the portrait of the Anointed Man, thus with a purpose permitted the human affections of His instrument to be seen, to show that perfect subjection to God could yet consist with what was truly human.

No less characteristic is the opening chapter. St. John, as befits him, begins with "the Word which was in the beginning, and was with God, and was God." And his tone throughout, not of this world, corresponds with the glory of the Only-begotten. Very different, but quite as perfect in its place, is the opening of this Gospel. It begins, like a simple tale touching the sons of men, with, "There was in the days of Herod the king a certain priest." And as it proceeds, we are introduced to human sympathies and relationships, in a way perfectly unlike anything we get in the other Gospels; with all the circumstances of the birth and infancy of the Holy Child, and of him who was sent as His forerunner. Here too, and here only, do we find the three inspired Songs, which, as speaking of mercy to Gentile as well as Jew, have for ages been the chosen utterance of the Church taken from among all nations. Here Mary sings, "He hath put down the mighty from their seat, and hath exalted them of low degree. He hath filled the hungry with good things, and the rich He hath sent empty away." Here even the priest looks beyond Israel, and while speaking of "salvation to his people," adds, "to give light to them that sit in darkness, and in the shadow of death"; while in the same strain the aged Simeon, ready to depart in peace, for his eyes have now seen God's salvation, cannot but add, that it is "prepared before the face of all people, a light to lighten the Gentiles, and to be the glory of Thy people Israel."

The second chapter is as distinctive. Beginning as usual here, with facts quite beyond the limits of the elect people, St. Luke notices that "in those days there went out a decree that all the world should be taxed." And then comes a fact which we should in vain look for in St. Matthew, that Joseph and Mary "went up to be taxed," among the rest who went every one to his own city. For the mind of the Spirit here is not so much to show One who has claims to rule, as One who is coming down perfectly on that ground which man as man then occupied.

Equally distinctive is the message of the angels to the watching shepherds. The kings of the East may ask in St. Matthew for One "who is born King." But in St. Luke the angel says, "Behold, I bring you good tidings of great joy, which shall be to all people; for unto you is born a Saviour: and this shall be the sign; Ye shall find the babe wrapped in swaddling clothes." After which we get the story of the infancy of "the Child": how "the Child grew"; how "the grace of God was on Him"; how "when He was twelve years old, He went up with His parents to Jerusalem to the feast"; how "the Child tarried behind, and His mother knew it not"; how "she said, Son, why hast Thou dealt thus"; how "He went down and was subject to them"; how "He increased in wisdom and stature, and in favor with God and man"; — these and points like these, as they are peculiar to this Gospel, distinctly mark our Lord as Man, personally entering man's lot, and Himself fully tasting it; joining Himself to us, in birth, in childhood, and in youth, that, being very Man, He might in His own blessed Person bring man near to God.

I trace the same tone throughout the next chapter, which records John's ministry, and the baptism of the Lord. It commences — for the Spirit is here occupied with man as such — with a glance over the world, the rulers of which, (for rulers are the key to the state of their subjects), are at some length given to us. Tiberius Caesar is reigning: Pontius Pilate governs Judea: Herod is tetrarch of Galilee: Philip of Iturea: Lysanias rules Abilene: while, (and this is not without purpose) two men are named as the high-priests of that people which had once been God's elect. Two high-priests in Israel — what a tale this told of the fall of the elect, who had become so mixed with the world, that where God had appointed one high-priest, the Gentile could now make many.* But this is characteristic, and in keeping here. The "Second Man" is to be seen, and men as they are, and their doings, are brought to show how God's thoughts are with them, even while their thoughts utterly differed from His thoughts. They have arranged the world as they like. Then He comes into the midst, both by His servants' preaching, and by His own life, to witness that what man now is, is opposed to God's image.

I have already noticed that in St. Matthew John comes preaching the "kingdom of heaven." Here he preaches "re-

---

* "In strict propriety there could be but one high-priest at a time, who held the office for life. But after the reduction of Judea to the Roman yoke, great changes were made, and the occupants of an office, which had enjoyed almost regal authority, were changed at the will of the conquerors. Hence some have supposed that the office had become annual, and that Annas and Caiaphas, occupying it by turns, each or both might be said to be the high priest" —*Bloomfield's Greek Testament,* in loco.

pentance for the remission of sins"; after which this Evangelist quotes the prophet, to show how in this act God was
opening the door, that "all flesh should see His salvation"
(Chap. 3:3, 6). Then here alone is the preaching of the
Baptist to men of every grade recorded. Here only do we
read, "The people asked him, saying, What shall we do?
— and the publicans said, What shall we do? — and the
soldiers likewise demanded of him, saying, And what shall
we do?" — all which inquiries here are answered with a
special word to each for man as man, whether soldier or
publican, is the object which the Spirit would here present
to us.

Then as to Christ's Baptism: here only do we read,
"When all the people were baptized, it came to pass, that
Jesus also being baptized, and praying, the heaven was
opened." He is linked here with "all the people," and it is
specially noted, that, being baptized, as becomes a Man
expressing His dependence, He "was praying." Baptism, as
shadowing death and resurrection, is specially connected
with us as sons of men, and also as members of that kingdom which flesh and blood cannot inherit. Therefore both
St. Matthew and St. Luke so fully record it; while St. John
for the same reason omits it, as being from the first occupied
with a view of Christ as the heavenly and only-begotten
Son.

Another fact, recorded only here, is that "Jesus now began to be about thirty years of age," a point of interest regarding Him as a man, and still more as a priest, if we take
the number "thirty" in its mystic signification. On this latter ground I scarce dare enter. A belief in mystic numbers
too often in these days only provokes a smile.* Nevertheless I am assured that this number, and indeed all else

---

* The thoughts of Augustine on this subject, as to the import and
value of mystic numbers as symbols, are well known. His 11th chap.
of the 2d book, *De Libero Arbitrio,* has some suggestive thoughts on
the subject. I confess I cannot see, why, if all creation be a type,
numbers alone should be excluded as having no signification. But
here as everywhere the seer is wanted.

which is distinctive here, is added with a special reason.
If I mistake not, it involves in type (as we know is the case
with other numbers, as for instance the number eight), the
very truth which was here set forth and fulfilled in Christ's
baptism. Baptism is burial and resurrection: "we are buried by baptism," because in Adam we are dead, and in this
act would confess our state, even while by faith in God's
love we claim through the death of self a higher lineage.
Christ as Son of Adam, through a mystic burial, figuring
that other baptism,* when all God's waves and billows went
over Him, here takes the place of Adam's Son, and thus
through death brings man into the higher relationship as
Son of God. Thus linking Himself with us in our shame,
He takes a place from whence henceforth He can meet the
vilest of Adam's children, and, because He has another life,
lift them up with Him into heavenly places. Thus this act
touches His priesthood: "for if He were on earth, He should
not be a priest, seeing there were priests who offered according to the law"(Heb. 8:4). But coming as He did in
baptism to ground where "heaven was opened" to Him,
He becomes, as the heavenly Man (thus anticipating His
resurrection), a fit High-priest for ruined men. Now the
thirtieth year in which the Jewish priest entered on his
office (Num. 4:3), like the eighth day of circumcision, fig-
ured this same mystery of death and resurrection, and as
such it is noticed here in the Gospel of the Son of Man; in
the letter speaking of His manhood; in the spirit, of a higher truth growing out of what as Man He did and suffered.

For a like reason, in this Gospel the genealogy is given at
His baptism, and not at His birth, to show us how the Son
of Adam claimed a higher lineage by mystic death and
resurrection. I need not notice that here the genealogy
is traced to Adam, and is, I doubt not, the mother's line,
to show, as was observed as long ago as the second century, that He whom St. Luke is showing us was very Man,

---

* "I have a baptism to be baptized with; and how am I straitened
until it be accomplished!" LUKE 12:50.

linked to, and about to head up afresh, all the families of
men who had sprung from the root of old Adam. All of
which is characteristic, and illustrative of the relationship
in which our Lord appears in this Gospel.

Equally marked is the account here given of the Lord's
opening ministry. Both St. Matthew and St. Mark notice the
fact, that after His baptism, "Jesus went into Galilee and
began to preach." But this Evangelist only gives the particulars, which are all characteristic. Here we read, "He
came to Nazareth, where He had been brought up." Then
in the Synagogue on the Sabbath-day He stood up to read
a scripture descriptive of Himself as the Anointed Man:
"The Spirit of the Lord is upon me, because the Lord hath
anointed me, . . . He hath sent me to heal the broken-hearted" (Chap. 4:16-18). All this is in keeping here. He goes
to the place "where He had been brought up," — "bringing
up" is a part of man's lot, — and confessing that "the Lord
has anointed Him," He declares the calling of the Gentiles,
preaching deliverance to captives, and good tidings to the
poor and broken-hearted.

Still more marked is the discourse which follows, which
is peculiar to St. Luke, where, in quoting the Old Testament, and showing how His course agreed with that of the
ancient prophets, He speaks of Elijah and Elisha, as being
sent, the one to Sarepta, a city of Sidon, to a widow there,
the other to Naaman the Syrian, that is to two Gentiles;
adding that remarkable declaration, so full of meaning,
that "no prophet is accepted in his own country"; words im-
plying that though rejected by the Jew, like Elijah and
Elisha, He should yet find poor widows and lepers among
the Gentiles, who would receive Him gladly.

These examples from the opening chapters of this Gospel may show how, while setting forth the Lord as Man,
the Spirit continually looks out to the Gentiles, on man as
man, far beyond elect Israel. And this peculiarity runs
throughout. Thus, in the 6th chapter, in that discourse
which answers in substance to the Sermon on the Mount,
here, not to dwell on the place and audience, is no refer-

ence to what "had been said of old time"; no allusion to
"the law and the prophets," as in St. Matthew's Gospel;
no correction of the errors of practiced religionists as to alms
and prayer; but simply broad moral teachings suited to the
state and wants of man as man. Many minor differences
might be noted, equally characteristic, as for instance, that
where St. Matthew writes, "Be ye therefore perfect, as your
Father in heaven is perfect," St. Luke recording another
form of the same expression (for doubtless the substance
of this Sermon was often repeated) says, "Be ye therefore
merciful, as you Father also is merciful"; thus putting His
disciples on the same ground He himself here occupies, as
coming down in mercy to meet the sons of men.

The same eye to man is seen in the mission of the Twelve
as given here. In St. Matthew their labors are specially
directed within the limits of a certain outward kingdom.
There we read that the Lord said, "Go not into the way of
the Gentiles, and into any city of the Samaritans enter ye
not; but go rather to the lost sheep of the house of Israel,
and as ye go, preach, saying, The kingdom of heaven is at
hand." St. Luke omits this, as beside his purpose, simply
saying, that "He sent them forth to preach," and that "they
departed, preaching the Gospel everywhere" (Chap. 9:6).
Then on their return this Evangelist records (the words are
only here and in St. Mark), that "John said, We saw one
casting out devils, and we forbade him, because he followeth not with us. And Jesus said, Forbid him not, for he that
is not against us is for us." St. Mark adds here, because it
bears on service, "For whosoever shall give you a cup of
water to drink in my name, because ye belong to Christ,
shall not lose his reward"(Mark 9:38-41).

St. Luke, while omitting this of the "cup of water," records the command, "Forbid him not," because it shows how
God may have a work among men outside of what we judge
to be the kingdom, with which disciples, if they are humble
and obedient, are not to strive or interfere. St. Luke then
adds a scene not elsewhere recorded but characteristic
here, as showing the heart of the Son of Man for men even

while they rejected Him. The disciples go into a village of the Samaritans to make ready for Him; "and they did not receive Him, because His face was as though He would go up to Jerusalem." At once the disciples, James and John, would have Him call for fire on the rejectors. Such is the flesh even in true and beloved followers of the loving Saviour — so unwilling to recognize laborers who are not with us; so ready to judge those who will not receive us. But Jesus turned and rebuked them, saying, "Ye know not what spirit ye are of; for the Son of Man is come, not to destroy men's lives, but to save them," — words omitted in the other Gospels, but perfect as revealing the Son of Man, who, with doors shut against Him, is yet content to bear this slight, if by long-suffering He may yet save lost sinners.

The mission of the Seventy, which immediately follows, and which is only here (Chap. 10:1ff.), is in the same tone, reaching forth as it does with manifest desire to win the sons of men. One little point here, peculiar to this Gospel, may perhaps be noticed. The Lord says, "Salute no man by the way"; and yet, "Into whatsoever house ye enter, say, Peace be to this house." The courtesies of life are not the chief thing with man in his present state. To be on good terms with those we meet is not the first thing, but rather, if it may be so, to set man right with God. To show how God's thoughts are thoughts of "peace," this is of far higher moment than salutations and greetings, which may only leave us far off from Him with whom we have to do.

Closely allied with this special regard for man as such, is the fact that throughout this Gospel in passages peculiar to St. Luke, man as he is, in his thoughts and ways, is searched and manifested in a truly wondrous manner. Take, for example, the particulars of the call of Peter as recorded here. This call is very briefly mentioned in the other Gospels; but here only do we read the exercises of Peter's heart; here only are we shown the feelings of a man, when for the first time he feels that God and His power are really brought near to him. He has been unsuccessful in fishing.

The Lord bids him let down the net. A great multitude of fish is at once caught, insomuch that the net broke. Then Peter is astonished, and falls down, and says, "Depart from me, for I am a sinful man, O Lord."

Many secrets of the heart are here. A little matter, a draught of fishes, some providential occurrence, and it may be very slight, at times flashes in upon a man whom the Lord is leading, making him feel that God is very near him. When this is the case, man at once discovers that he is sinful, and as such would have the glory, which shows him his littleness, to depart from him. All this, as it is peculiar here, is quite in keeping, as showing man as he is.* Similar in character are the other words, only recorded in this same chapter, that "No man, having drunk old wine, straightway desireth new; for he saith, The old is better." The scene generally, and the conversation touching "new wine and old bottles," is in three of the Gospels; but here only are we carefully told the effect produced by drinking the old wine. In this another secret of human nature is disclosed, as to the power of habit and association to affect and bind the soul of man. If we indulge ourselves with the old wine, the excitements of the flesh, the new wine of the kingdom will not be relished by us. He that drinks the old will not desire the new; indeed, while the savor of the old remains, though the new far surpasses the old, he will yet say, "The old is better." St. Luke, and it is perfect here where man is the object before the mind of the Spirit, gives us, in what is peculiar to his Gospel, many fine touches of this nature which, for this same reason are omitted by St.

---

* I just note here that some have objected that the call of the Apostles, as recorded in St. John, is not the same as that recorded by the other three Evangelists. I believe it is not. But such as have themselves been called, and experientially know all these steps, know also that we, like the disciples of old, are called distinctly several times; first in one place, when we are John's disciples, (John 1:37-42;) after which we yet cling to our nets, and need another call (Luke 5:1-10) to bring us to walk with Jesus. We may require yet another, when the cross is seen in all its bitterness. (John 21:3, 19).

Matthew and St. Mark, as lying out of that special line which it was their office to present to us.

Having thus shown how broadly the Spirit through this Gospel looks out on man, I would now throw together several particulars, only noticed in this Gospel, and equally characteristic, as to the ways and conduct of the Pattern Man.

And here the first point I will notice is, that throughout this Gospel, again and again, in scenes common to the other Evangelists, and where they say nothing of prayer, St. Luke repeatedly adds, that "He was praying"; and this because, as prayer adds to the perfectness of the picture as Man, the Evangelist would show how "the Man Christ Jesus" continually exercised this grace of true dependence. Thus here only do we read, that at His baptism He *"was praying"*: here only that when he had cleansed the leper, "He withdrew Himself, *and prayed"* (Chap. 5:12, 16). So again, here only are we told that His choice of the twelve followed a night of ceaseless prayer: "He continued *all night in prayer,* and when it was day, He called His disciples unto Him, and of them He chose twelve." So again, here only do we read that Peter's famous confession was made *"as Jesus was alone praying."* Here only are we told that the Transfiguration happened as He prayed: "He went up into a mountain, and as *He prayed,* the fashion of His countenance was changed." So again, in this Gospel, the Lord's Prayer was given, in answer to a request from His disciples, who, *"as He was praying,* when He ceased said, Lord, teach us to pray." In St. Matthew our Lord repeats this in His Sermon on the Mount, teaching us not to be ashamed to reiterate the self-same words, if only they are good words, in the ears of our disciples.

I may also note here, for it is characteristic, that in St. Luke, in the Lord's Prayer, we have, "Forgive us our *sins,"* instead of "Forgive us our *debts,"* as in St. Matthew's Gospel. And trifling as the difference may appear, the instructed eye will see how perfectly it accords with the distinctive character of the respective Gospels; *"debts"* being the thought as connected with a kingdom, where righteousness is the rule; *"sins,"* where men generally are regarded, who without law are yet sinners. Again in this Gospel only have we the words of Peter, *"I have prayed for thee"* (Chap. 22:32). All of which, as it is peculiar here, is not only characteristic of the Lord as very Man, but a deeply instructive example of what becomes us as sons of men, to whom every event, be it baptism, or ministry, or social intercourse, the choice of preachers, or the hour of rest, each and all should be an occasion of renewed communion with God, with prayer not only for our own souls, but also for those of others.

Another point equally characteristic is the care this Evangelist takes to record circumstances illustrative of the Human sympathy of our Lord, not given in the other Gospels. Thus in the scene with the widow of Nain (Chap. 7:11-16), which is peculiar to St. Luke, the Evangelist notes some particulars which would naturally affect a tender human heart. The young man who had died was *"the only son* of his mother," and *"she was a widow";* for human sorrows and affections here are all noted. Then when Jesus saw her, *"He had compassion on her";* and when He had raised the youth, *"He delivered him to his mother,"* as One, who having known a mother's love, could truly feel with her. And I may note here that in scenes common to the other Gospels, St. Luke, by the addition of a single word, touches a human chord, beautifully in character with that view which it is his special work to present to us. For instance, in the case of Jarius' daughter, St. Luke alone tells us that she was his *"only"* child. So where another father comes to seek help, here only are his words recorded, "For he is *mine only child."* Such a fact would touch a Man, and as such we find it here, revealing the perfect sympathy of Him "who is not ashamed to call us brethren."

Equally distinctive is the repeated mention, so often found in this Gospel, of the fact that our Lord "sat down to eat meat." He is here eminently a social Man, going to tables where He is asked, and there, whether in houses of Publicans or Pharisees, using that social intercourse to instruct others. Thus He sanctifies man's commonest engagements and needs, for man must eat; showing us how even the lower necessities of our bodies may be made occasions of ministering the bread of life. How He sits at table is fully seen here. A Pharisee invites Him and He goes; but even while at table He is occupied with a poor sinner, though His compassion for her provokes the assembled guests to judge Him, first as profane, and then as arrogant. At table, and in another's house, He fills the hungry with good things, while the rich, satisfied with themselves, are sent away empty. And this scene, recorded only here, full of the workings of man's heart, is perfectly in keeping with the special tenor of this Gospel; showing us that not merit or righteousness, but a sense of sin, is the fit introduction to Him who came to save sinners.

I notice here too, that in this Gospel the Lord repeats at table a great portion of that teaching, which, as we know from St. Matthew, was elsewhere given in public and set sermons. His audience is changed, but not His doctrine; in fact, the very words are adhered to, as if by this means He would the more firmly fix them on His disciples' hearts.*
At a Pharisee's table, Pharisees are reproved. The fact that He is an invited guest shall not keep Him from faithfully warning those with whom He sits of the woes consequent on a form of godliness without the power.

Take another example of His manner at table, quite pe-

---

* Many instances are recorded of our Lord uttering nearly the same words on different occasions: as the words, "I will have mercy and not sacrifice," twice recorded in St. Matthew. (Chap. 9:13, and 12:7). So the answer to the repeated charge that "He cast out devils through Beelzebub" (Matt. 9:34, and 12:24). So the repeated references to His cross in almost the self-same words. (Matt. 16:21, 17:23, 20:17, 19). So in St. Matthew He uttered the Lord's Prayer in His Sermon on the Mount. In St. Luke, we find He gave it with some slight alteration to His disciples in reply to a request that He would teach them to pray. Every teacher knows how often he has used the same words to different audiences, and with slight differences. Our Lord did the same, as many places in the Gospels plainly intimate.

culiar to St. Luke, but showing how blessedly He used for the good of men those social seasons which we so often misuse to our own injury; revealing too that blessed heart, which, while so keenly alive to man's needs, at the same time most deeply felt the contradiction of man's wickedness and selfishness on every side. A Pharisee asks Him to dine, and He accepts the call (Chap. 14:1ff.). It was "the Sabbath-day," and He knew they "watched Him"; but though conscious that any service on that day would bring on Him reproach, He nevertheless stops, as He enters the door, to heal a poor sufferer. Then, as He goes to dinner, He cannot but mark how "those who were bidden," chose the best places. Self is at work; human nature comes out even in so small a thing as a seat at table. For this He has a word. Then at the table, the choice of the guests suggests much. Men invite their rich neighbors, for they expect recompense. This draws for His comments. Then one at the table, "as he heard these things," apparently touched by the thought of that day, when poor and rich should all be brought together, said, "Blessed is he that shall eat meat in the kingdom of God."

At once the Lord seems carried in spirit from the table before Him, for seats at which the guests are so eager, to another feast, which is prepared, and yet despised by men; from attendance at which they beg to be excused. The thought that when man spreads a table, it is full, contrasts strangely with the truth, that when God makes a feast, not one of the guests who are only bidden care to come. To sup with God, they must be compelled. But I need not pursue this. The whole scene, as it is peculiar to St. Luke, shows not only what man is, but what man has been in Christ Jesus, who, "whether He ate or drank," was recollected, doing all to the glory of God, while His heart yet yearned over the sons of men.

I have as yet said nothing of the Parables peculiar to St. Luke, save that in their opening form they remarkably differ from those in St. Matthew's Gospel. Here it is always, — "A certain man." "A certain man fell among

thieves" — "A certain man had a fig-tree planted in his
vineyard" — "A certain man made a great supper" — "What
man of you, having a hundred sheep, if he lose one of them,
will not leave the ninety and nine in the wilderness?" — or
"What woman having ten pieces of silver, if she lose one
piece, will not seek diligently till she find it?" So in the
Parable of the Prodigal Son, "A certain man had two sons."
So again, "There was a certain rich man which had a stew-
ard." So again, "There was a certain man clothed in purple
and fine linen." So again, "Two men went up into the temple to pray." These parables are peculiar to St. Luke, and
in their contents, as in their form, show the Lord as looking out broadly on man, more especially on man as lost
and yet cared for. To take only the first, the Good Samaritan. Here it is seen how a Stranger can do for the ruined
what Priest and Levite cannot. Priests served for the pure
in the temple; but here is One who can meet even those
who, going down from Jerusalem to the cursed city of
Jericho (Josh. 6:26), have been left sorely wounded. I need
not speak of such parables as those in the well-known 15th
chapter, where God's own joy in saving the lost is so won-
drously revealed to us; or of those which inculcate prayer
(Chap. 11:5ff. and 18:1ff.), which, as they are peculiar
here, pointedly mark man's place as a dependent creature.

Generally speaking, in all these parables, whether we
regard their mere letter or their hidden spirit, a careful
eye will see God's will respecting man, in some cases His
special purpose to Gentiles in contrast with Jews. This,
among other instances, is seen in the way in which two
parables given by St. Matthew are here placed in a
connection exactly in keeping with the object of St. Luke's
Gospel. In St. Matthew the "Leaven" and "Mustard-seed"
come as as part of a series, describing the development of
the mystery of the kingdom; here they come in immediately after the parable of the Barren Fig-tree, from which for
three years fruit was sought in vain, and which was threat-
ened with the axe if in the fourth year there should be no
increase: showing how, when the tree of Judaism should

be felled, the Sower's work in the field, and the leavening of the lump, would begin, all exactly in character here, where the Spirit looks beyond Jewish ground to the work among men coming in on Israel's failure. But all this is perfectly in keeping with the veiw of Christ as Son of Adam.

To the peculiarities already noticed I might add many more, such as the fact that here only we have allusion to *"the times of the Gentiles";* here only do we read of "Jerusalem being trodden down *of the Gentiles,"* and her people "led away captive into *all nations* (Chap. 21:24). Here only the shooting of the fig-tree is seen with *"all the trees."* Here only is the place of crucifixion called by its Gentile name, *"Calvary,"* rather than, as in the other Gospels, Golgotha. Here only is the dying thief seen as saved by grace, in beautiful harmony with the whole tenor of this Gospel. So as to the Lord. Here only in the Garden is "an angel seen strengthening Him," to show how truly He was Man, receiving angels' ministry. Here only do we read of "the bloody sweat": here only does He say to the traitor, "Judas, betrayest thou *the Son of Man* with a kiss?" Here only does the Centurion say, "This was *a righteous Man."* Here only on the cross does the Lord as a Man *"commend His spirit"* into the hands of God, His Father. So here only, after His resurrection He eats with men, verifying His manhood by yet partaking of "a piece of broiled fish and of a honey-comb." But all this, and much more of a like nature, will meet the attentive reader, and illustrate that distinct view of the Lord which is here presented to us.

And now one word on the bearing of these things on us, who are Adam's sons. Need I draw out the moral of the repeated reference to prayer in this Gospel? Did the Son of Man pray at His baptism, when He chose apostles, when alone — did His prayer lead others to say, "Teach us to pray also"; and shall we who have nothing in ourselves be yet prayerless? Did He at table make every circumstance an occasion of blessed and holy teaching, and shall we not strive, after His pattern, to eat to God's glory, to sit in social circles, diffusing something of His Spirit to all around?

Oh! may we but see Him as He is, that like Him in the midst of men, instead of being affected by them, we may affect them in the power of a Higher Presence. And let us, who, though sons of Adam, by union with our risen Head, are conscious of possessing another and higher calling — who have confessed ourselves dead and risen, with heaven opened, and who, "by baptism, fasting, and temptation," are longing to be conformed to Him who went before — see that these things which were true in Him may be true in us also, for "as He is, so are we in this world."

And if there be some, as, alas! there are, who know not man's calling, as chosen in Christ to be the heir of all things, let them, looking in the face of Jesus, see God's love to man, who so loved us that He gave His Son to be for us a Perfect Man; to be borne in the womb, to be born, to hang upon a woman, to suck her breasts, to be taught by her lips, to increase in wisdom here; to know our relationships, and our sorrows, and our toils, and at last our death, that in everything He might be linked with us, and through His death, still not losing us, might in Himself lift us up, to sit in heavenly places — angels, and principalities, and powers, all subject to Him as Man, a pledge that to us also they shall be subject in due season. Oh, might the mystery of His Incarnation come home to us as befits its glory! Oh, that we might understand what it witnesses of God's purpose touching the sons of men; that He should be our everlasting dwelling-place, and we His temples; that He should be seen in us, and we be hid in Him!

May the word, spoken by angels, "To you is born a Saviour," remove every doubt, if such can yet remain, as to the love of Him who thus loved us. "To you is born a Saviour." It is a birth-relationship, true whether we own and rejoice in it, or put it away from us. We have nothing to do to make Him a Saviour: He is "born a Saviour": He is a Man, and nothing pertaining to man can now be alien to Him. What should we think of the child, who, when told, "To you is born a brother," should answer, "But what shall I do to make him a brother to me?" The joy is, He is born a Brother, by birth linked to us, that we through grace might henceforth in Spirit be linked with Him. We may indeed deny the bond, and live groaning here as though God had never so loved man as to make him His son in Christ Jesus. We may doubt His love. Nevertheless "to us a Son is born"; and we who have trusted know that through and in Him is perfect peace.

While, therefore, we rejoice to trace the wisdom, seen even in the form of that revelation, which God in His rich grace has given to us, let none be content intellectually to trace this detail, unless with this, from His inmost heart he also embraces Him of whom this Gospel speaks. The wisdom of God in grace as in nature may be coldly contemplated, like any other piece of skill or wondrous workmanship, without a soul-saving and personal appropriation of the grace, which is yet by the understanding discerned so clearly. But, as one has said, "the Gospel has not been revealed that we may have the pleasure of feeling or expressing fine sentiments, but that we may be saved: the taste may receive the impression of the beauty and sublimity of the Bible, and the nervous system may have received the impression of the tenderness of its tone, and yet its meaning, its deliverance, its mystery of holy love, may remain all unknown."

PRAYER

Almighty God, who hast given us Thine Only-begotten Son, to take our nature upon Him, and for us to be born of a pure Virgin, grant that we, being regenerate, and made Thy children by adoption and grace, may daily be renewed by Thy Holy Spirit, through the same our Lord Jesus Christ, who liveth and reigneth with Thee, and the same Spirit, ever one God, world without end. *Amen.*

John's View

"The fourth living creature was like a flying Eagle" REV. 4:7.
"The way of an Eagle in the air is too wonderful for me" PROV. 30:18.

WE COME NOW TO THAT GOSPEL which more than any other carries on its face the plainest tokens of being occupied with an aspect of Christ distinct from all the rest. "The fourth living creature was like unto an eagle." And if in tracing those views of the Lord, the emblems of which are taken from creatures which walk on earth, it has been difficult to bring within my limits the characteristic peculiarities of each Gospel, what shall I say of this Gospel, which like the eagle soars away to heaven, where nearly the whole is peculiar, and every part throughout replete with mysteries touching the Son of God? Canst thou fly as the eagle? "She mounteth up on high: she dwelleth and abideth in the rock, upon the strong place. Her eyes behold afar off; her young ones suck up blood, and where the slain is, there is she" (Job 39:27). Who can follow here? Some have heard a voice, saying, "I bare you upon eagles' wings" (Exod. 19:4): and in His strength who makes His redeemed to ride upon high places, they also "mount up with wings as eagles" (Isa. 40:31). For "as an eagle stirreth up her nest, fluttereth over her young, spreadeth abroad her wings, taketh them, beareth them on her wings; so the Lord leads His beloved" into heavenly places, thence to behold what such as walk on earth can never see.

But alas! how little have we seen, how little are we fit to see, the precious things which are above this world. And yet it is this that St. John treats of, revealing the Lord

as "not of this world," for the contemplation of those who
like Him are not of this world; in tones replete with heav-
en, and which are themselves everywhere the exact echo
of that Blessed One of whom they speak; witnessing how
deeply His image and Spirit had sunk down into and per-
vaded the whole soul of "that disciple whom Jesus loved."

My present purpose, however, is rather to indicate than to
explore the subject; to show that there is a special purpose
here, rather than to attempt to fathom its great deep. For
here we may bathe our souls in seas of rest; here we indeed
come to waters far above the loins or ankles: "the waters
are risen, waters to swim in, a river that cannot be passed
over." Having therefore briefly shown, though indeed it
needs no proof, how remarkably this Gospel differs from
the rest, I would endeavor to learn some of the lessons
which these peculiarities are intended to impress upon us.

To turn then to this Gospel. How distinctive is its beginning. Omitting the birth of Jesus as Son of Man, St.
John begins before all worlds. "In the beginning was the
Word, and the Word was with God, and the Word was
God." Then comes the wondrous announcement, that
though "all things were made by Him, and without Him was
not anything made that was made"; though "in Him was
Life, and the Life was the Light," yet "He was made flesh
and dwelt among us." For man had departed from God,
and lost His image. Then "the image of God" (Col. 1:15)
comes to dwell in man, that man may dwell in God. No
man could see God: therefore the Only-begotten Son, who
is in the bosom of the Father, came to declare Him to
us. All this, and much more of a like nature, which meets
us at the opening of this Gospel, is too remarkable to escape observation. Instead of the Lord of a kingdom, here
it is "The Light of men." Instead of a Servant, here we see
"Him who made all things." Instead of a Man subject to
the powers of this world, born of a woman, laid in a man-
ger, here it is "the Only-begotten Son, who is in the bosom
of the Father," revealing His image, and communicating life
"to as many as received Him" among the sons of men. Ob-

jections may be raised, and explanations offered, but the
fact is beyond all doubt, that the views here rises, as the
heaven is above the earth, over which any which is given
to us in the other Gospels.

Equally characteristic is the notice of John. The Baptist
is elsewhere seen rather in connection with the earthly
than the heavenly relations of the Lord Jesus. Here it
is clear that the Evangelist sees more, and wishes more
to be seen in him, than the man. If Jesus is "the Light,"
John is also a light, though of another nature; a "lamp,
burning and shining," yet but a lamp,* destined to be
quenched soon as the Light of heaven shall have introduced
the perfect day. So Jesus is "the Word" here, and John
is "the Voice;" words, which even partially apprehended,
convey something to us very different from such titles as
"the Lord," and "my Messenger." The "Word" (Logos)
is the sense: the "Voice" is the sound. Outwardly, the voice
seems to be first, yet while in the act of communication
it precedes the word, it is not really before it, for the
sense must have been in the mind before it was out-
spoken. So the word, if it has been received, abides in
the heart; but the voice passes away. Having served to
communicate the word, which was in one heart to other
hearts, the voice has done its work. Its use is as a witness,
and this being accomplished, the word remains, while
the witnessing voice is content to be forgotten. All this,
as it applies to Him who is "the Word," and His forerunner, has been noticed by saints in other days.* To some
it may be a hint of what is here for such as through

---

* Chap. 5:35. The contrast between Christ as *the Light,* and John
as *the lamp,* is lost in the common version, where the words respecting John, *ekeinos en ho luchnos ho kaiomenos,* have been rendered,
"He was a burning *light.*" The Vulgate here more correctly gives,
"Ille erat *lucerna* ardens."

* Augustine again and again refers to the mystery contained in
the fact, that Christ is "*the Word,*" and John "*the Voice.*" A reference
to the following passages will amply repay perusal, and suggest much:
Serm. 288, § 2 and 3; *Serm.* 289, § 3; *Serm.* 293, § 3.

grace can receive it. To all it speaks of the Lord in a
relation connected with heaven rather than with earth.

No less distinctive is the witness of the Baptist, as
recorded here. In St. Matthew he preaches a "coming
kingdom;" in St. Luke "repentance;" while here he is "a
witness to the Light, that all men through him might believe" (Chap. 1:7). Accordingly that part of his witness
which is given here, touches the heavenly side of the
Lord: — "I saw and bear record that this is the Son of
God." "Again, the next day, John stood and two of His
disciples, and looking upon Jesus as He walked, he said,
Behold the Lamb of God" (Chap. 1:32-36). All this, so
perfectly in keeping here, is passed in silence by the
other Evangelists, who, as their office is to show the Human rather than the Divine in Christ, (though in a sense
even the Human in Him is all Divine), record such parts
of the Baptist's testimony as bear upon their respective
views, while St. John selects what is more connected with
the Divine nature. How this testimony touches those who
are "partakers of the Divine nature," we may see presently.
Suffice it to notice here how the particulars given by St.
John all lead us to contemplate the Son of God.

The Baptist's words, too, respecting himself, as given
here, which at first sight appear opposed to what St.
Matthew has recorded of him, like all such apparent
contradictions, express a deep truth, experimentally known
by all who, like John, have been called by grace to "prepare the way of the Lord" by the preaching of His gospel. In St. Matthew John the Baptist says to Christ, "I
have need to be baptized of Thee, and comest Thou to
me" (Matt. 3:14); whereas in St. John he says, "I knew
Him not, but He that sent me to baptize with water, the
same said unto me, Upon whom thou shalt see the Spirit
descending, and remaining upon Him, the same is He
which baptizeth with the Holy Spirit. And I saw and
bare record that this is the Son of God" (Chap. 1:33, 34).
Carelessly heard, these words do seem to have a dis-
crepancy. But once see that St. John is speaking of our

Lord in an aspect as much higher than St. Matthew's view
as the Eternal Word is higher than the Son of David and
Abraham, and then the words, which to our darkness may
seem dark, in His light will yield only more brightness.
For we may know, and do know, Christ as Son of David,
and as such the rightful Heir of great glory long before
we know Him as the Word, who gives the Holy Spirit. I
speak what I have known and felt. And I know that from
the first of my witness to Christ, when like John I went
preaching and baptizing, I so far knew Christ as to say,
"I have need to be. baptized of Thee;" for even then I
saw He was Lord of a kingdom, and that I more needed
to be baptized of Him, than He could need my poor
testimony; and yet I knew Him not as the Word, until,
in the act of receiving Him, that I might bear witness of
Him, the Father revealed Him to me in such a character as I had till then never known or conceived of; and
this, though from my youth I had been taught to believe
that Jesus was the Son of God; so that I can truly say, "I
knew Him not;" while yet from the first I knew that I had
"need to be baptized of Him." And this high knowledge
of Christ as the Eternal Word — a knowledge we at first
have not — is that of which St. John is speaking, and which
is the special burden of this Gospel. But here, as in all
things, experience only makes clear. "We must do the
works, if we would know of the doctrine" (Chap. 7:17).

The next chapter — and it is one of a series, each stage
of which illustrates some virtue of the Son — is full
of particulars equally characteristic. Could I speak of the
mysteries hid under the letter here, this would be yet more
manifest. Here the first lesson is, that man's work ever
ends in failure, while the work of the Son, out of man's
failure, brings in yet greater glory. "Every man" — this
is the way of men, in opposition to the way of the Son, —
"Every man at the beginning sets forth good wine:" nature
and the world give their best and fairest at the beginning;
"but when men have well drunk, then that which is worse."
Not so with the Son of God. "Thou hast kept the best

wine until now." When man's feast fails, there yet remains what the Son of God has in store for them who
bid Him welcome. And though with men the first is best,
not so with the Son of God. His good wine comes sweeter
and sweeter even to the end (Chap. 2:10). The same
truth comes out touching the temple. Man may, and will,
ruin what he can; but the Son shall raise it up in greater
glory.° But even the letter here is distinctive. "The
mother of Jesus saith unto Him, They have no wine. Jesus
saith unto her, (could such words be found in St. Luke?)
Woman, what have I to do with thee?" Then we read,
"This beginning of miracles did Jesus in Cana of Galilee,
and manifested forth His glory;" for though the veil was
yet upon Him, "the glory as of the Only begotten" could
not be wholly hid. So of the temple of His body, He says
here, — for "the Son quickeneth whom He will," — "Destroy this temple, and I will raise it up" (Chap. 2:4, 11,
19). So we read, "Jesus did not commit Himself unto
them, because He knew all men, and needed not that any
should testify of man; for He knew what was in man," —
words, which, as they bring to our remembrance the prophet's witness, "The heart is deceitful, who can know it?"
and the answer, "I the Lord search the heart," reveal
Jesus as the Lord, "to whom all hearts are open, all desires
known, and from whom no secrets are hid." But this is
exactly in keeping with that view which is now before us,
of "the Word who was with God, and who was God."

Even more marked is the next chapter, where the

° Chap. 2:19. Strauss, while discussing the charge brought against
the Lord, that He had said, "I will destroy this temple," etc., and
not'ng the fact that St. Luke omits this, says, with his usual effrontery,
"It is highly probable that the declaration about the destruction and
rebuilding the temple was really uttered by Jesus. *That Luke omits
the production of the false witnesses is therefore to be regarded as a
deficiency in h:s narrative.*" (Vol. iii. p. 214). This judge of the
Gospels cannot see how what is perfectly in keeping touching the
Son of God may be out of character in the description of the *Son of
Man.* Surely the wisdom of this world is foolishness with God.

doctrine of a "second birth," as connected with Himself, "the Only-begotten Son of God," is given in a tone quite different from anything in the other Gospels. We have here an advance on the preceding chapter. There generally it was shown how, when man's work ended in failure, the Son out of that failure could bring in better things; a fit introduction to the miracles of grace to be accomplished by the Son of the Father. Here the detail of that special miracle, (occupying the following chapter,) of the indwelling of the Holy Spirit. With Nicodemus, the subject is "the birth of water and the Spirit." With the woman of Samaria, it is "the well of water within, springing up unto everlasting life."

And here I would observe — for these scenes with Nicodemus, and the Samaritan, are examples — that in St. John though facts are related they are never, as in the other Gospels, recorded for their own sakes, but invariably serve to introduce some spiritual discourse, of which the fact is generally the outward sign: the discourse or doctrine being invariably introduced with "Verily, verily," an expression not to be found in any of the other Gospels. This very form of the Gospel is characteristic. We saw something like this in St. Luke, where describing the Son of Man, the very style, so distinctly human, was suited to the subject which that Evangelist had to set before us. The tendency in St. John to rise to heaven, and to witness of heavenly things, is no less marked, and is equally in keeping with that view of the Lord, which it is his office to present to us.

As to the details of the interview with Nicodemus, I may add a word, for the truth here, growing out of that relationship of the Lord, which is set forth in this Gospel, is of the most vital interest. How is man to become God's son? This is the question here; and a fit question to have an early place in the Gospel which reveals the Son of God. In baptism indeed the Lord in His own person had shown the path, but its mystery had as yet never been opened out. Here the secret is told. Natural birth will

bring us into this world; but natural birth will not introduce us into the kingdom which is within the veil. To
go thither we must be re-born. But how can this be? The
wise Pharisee, who comes regarding the Lord as "a teacher,"
and commencing his discourse with a self-sufficient "We
know," is forced to confess he knows nothing, and to
cry, "How can these things be?" before the mystery of the
new-birth can be revealed to him. To be re-born we want
something more than "a teacher." As sons of men, our
life and portion is of the earth, earthly. Unfit for heaven,
careless of its joys, how shall man enter there? Can the
flesh be changed to bear the Lord's presence? "That which
is born of the flesh is flesh;" and "flesh and blood cannot
inherit the kingdom." What then can be done? There
must be the communication of another life. So the Son
who is the Word, "in whom is life," came down to men,
and laid hold of man in His own Person. He entered the
kingdom of this world, and became a Man, that so laying
hold of man, and traversing the length and breadth of
man's portion, He might lift man, as quickened by Him,
through death into another life, as God's heir, and Christ's
joint-heir. Therefore we are baptized. We come as dead
ones, confessing that our life as men is utterly unfit to give
us admission into the Lord's presence. We come to put off
that life, and are buried in baptism, renouncing Old Adam,
to claim a new life in union with the life-giving Word;
in the faith that if He be in us, His home shall be ours,
and though for a season we yet bear the image of the
earthy, we shall also bear the image of the heavenly. This
in effect is what the Lord says here. Ye must be born
again. Do you ask, How can these things be? How can
man rise up to enter heaven? No man can ascend thither,
save He that came down from heaven, even the Son of
Man which is in heaven. But to take man thither He has
come to take man's lot and die. For as the serpent was
lifted up, so shall the Son of Man be lifted up. Then faith
in Him, risen and ascended, shall bring others to Him,
and they who receive the Word shall live with Him. Thus

by the reception of the Word, man receives a life as real and much more blessed than the natural life he has in old Adam — a life which exists the witness that judgment is in one sense behind us, for Jesus is risen, and our regeneration is a participation in His resurrection and eternal life. Thus does "the lifting up of the Son" close all earthly associations, and introduce to heavenly things hitherto all unknown. I cannot do more than touch the question here; but the whole passage is a marked example of the tone which runs through this Gospel. Indeed the words repeated so often — "He that believeth on the Son hath everlasting life" — sufficiently show what is the mind of the Spirit in this Scripture. "Cursed is the man that trusteth in man, and maketh flesh his arm" (Jer. 17:5). But "he that believeth on the Son hath everlasting life."

And here let me observe how this word *"life,"* so repeatedly recurring here,* contrasts with the language of St. Matthew's Gospel. With St. Matthew the idea throughout is *"righteousness,"* rather than *"life."* Of course life and righteousness are but different forms or expressions of one and the same reality. But where St. Matthew, as befits his view of "the kingdom," sees righteousness, St. John sees life. Thus St. Matthew, as I have already noticed, records the words, "Suffer it to be so now, for thus it becometh us to fulfil all righteousness." St. John testifies of the Only-begotten, — "In Him was life, and the life was the light of men." And this contrast runs through the Gospels. The Epistles have the like distinction. For instance, "righteousness" is the form of expression peculiar to the first Epistle. But where Paul says, "The righteousness of God without the law was manifested," John still in character, says, "The life was manifested." Where Paul comes to "declare God's righteousness, that He might be just, and yet a justifier," John comes "to bear witness, and show unto you that eternal life, which was with the Father, and was manifested to us." Both speak of the same reality,

---

* See Chap. 3:36; 5:26, 29, 40; 6:33, 35, 48, 51, 53, 63, etc.

in different forms, not without a reason; even as the difference of form in the Gospels develops the fulness of the same blessed Lord.

The following chapter, of the woman of Samaria, takes up the same strain, enlarging on the growth and nourishment of the new life through faith in Christ Jesus. Nicodemus is told of the *quickening*, the Samaritan woman of the *indwelling* of life, through that Spirit, whose work it is to testify of and glorify the Son of God. The religious Jew is chosen to show that in spite of all his religion, he needs new life. The defiled Samaritan to be a witness that, in spite of all her sins, even in her soul there might be a well of living water. Here faith in the Son gives "a well of water springing up into everlasting life;" making us, now that we are alive, "worshippers," not in certain earthly places, but "in spirit and in truth"; revealing to us "the Father" as "seeking such to worship Him"; and enabling us to worship Him in the spirit of dear children. And all this, not in virtue of anything in man, for here one of the vilest is the example chosen to show us where this grace may find its dwelling, but as springing from union with the Son: — "The water which I shall give," is that which transforms this lost one, and others like her, into a vessel, first to contain, then to minister, the grace of life.

The next three chapters rise yet higher, with a witness to the Person of the Son, the force of which I despair of expressing, even in the measure which has flashed in upon my own soul. I may however observe that in these three chapters, (5-7) the Lord is contrasted with all that law or ordinances had done for God's elect. Nay, He is shown as the fulfilment of all, whether Sabbaths, Passovers, or the like, Himself the true rest and food for weary souls. The way in which these feasts are set aside here, to lead us higher, is very striking. Each of these chapters begins with a reference to some solemnity once ordained by God Himself; first, the Sabbath; then the Passover; then the

Feast of Tabernacles.* These were forms, the witness of what God had done, or would do, for ruined men. Once the forms had glorified God, being used as seals of His truth, to give both to God and man their due place. Then there was life in them for men. But the time had come when these same forms were used to glorify men, to make sinners of one class glory over sinners of another, and then all was death. Then the Word, coming in a form in which God was glorified, through which therefore there was life for men, set Himself in contrast to the forms mis-used to glorify man, and which for this reason had become powerless. And they who clung to the form, all the more strongly because they lacked the life, fought against the life in Him, making the very form their weapon to resist that of which it was the witness. Nevertheless there stood the Vessel, in which God was glorified, and which there-fore ministered rest and life to weary men, declaring that not only from Himself, the Only-begotten, but from those who believed in Him, and were adopted children, living waters should flow to comfort those around, when He was glorified. One in the form of a Man, glorifying God on earth, was here saying, "If any man thirst, let him come unto me and drink:" nay more, saying of His disciples, "He that believeth on me, out of his belly shall flow rivers." And "this spake He of the Spirit, which they that believe on Him should receive, for the Holy Spirit was not yet given, because that Jesus was yet glorified" (Chap. 7:37-39). O wondrous truth, that from the temples of our bodies, if only the Lord and not self is glorified, there shall run "living waters"; while if self is exalted, spite of all our knowledge, not one drop shall be ministered by us to weary souls! We may be believers, and yet the

---

* Chapter 5 begins, "After this there was a feast of the Jews" (v. 1). That this was *the Sabbath,* appears from v. 9. Chapter 6 commences, "And *the Passover,* a feast of the Jews, was nigh" (6:4). In chapter 7:2, we read, "Now the Jew's *feast of Tabernacles* was at hand.

Lord may not in us be glorified. We may yet be under
law, not come even to the cross, much less to Pentecost;
nay, we may be crucifying Him afresh, and putting Him
to an open shame. In such a case the Holy Spirit will not
be given, because Jesus is not yet·glorified. Where He is
glorified, though Pharisees and the world rage and imagine
vain things, the living waters shall run into the desert,
and "everything shall live wither the river comes."

My limits forbid my tracing, as I would desire, the
truths unfolded here, as linked with the Person of the
Lord, as Son of God. I may however observe, for it is
characteristic of this Gospel, that the 5th chapter, which
speaks of the work on the Sabbath, a work wrought as
our Lord says, because neither God nor man could rest
in sin and misery,* contrasts the incompetency of law,
which, like the pool of Bethesda, required something
of strength in the patient, with the absolute life-giving
power of the Son of God; showing in addition that if
men will not receive Him as Life-giver, they must as
Judge; that in one or other of these relations He must be
known by all men. The 6th chapter shows His place on
earth, according to the mystery of the Paschal Lamb; that
He must suffer, and yet give life to men; fulfilling the
word, "He shall satisfy her poor with bread;" then opening to His disciples the secret of that Bread which came
down from heaven; and then concluding with the question, "What and if ye shall see the Son of Man ascend

---

* The Lord's words were, "My Father worketh hitherto, and I
work." As though He had said, You judge me for breaking the Sabbath in healing this sufferer on the Sabbath-day. I do so because it
has been proved — this man's misery proves it — that this Sabbath,
the rest of the first creation, is indeed no Sabbath. There is no rest
in it now either for God or man, for neither God nor man can rest in
sin and misery. God did indeed rest in an unfallen world, and since
the fall, before finally giving up the first creation to condemnation,
He tried it once and again; giving, while the trial lasted, the Sabbath
as a sign of a rest in the first creation. But sin works in it, and God
cannot rest. Therefore, instead of "God *did rest* the seventh day,"
the truth now is, "My Father *worketh* hitherto, and I work."

up where He was before" (Chap. 6:62)? After this comes
the instruction of the 7th chapter, touching the Feast of
Tabernacles, where, having testified that the time for His
manifestation to the world as Son of Man was not yet
come, He comes as the Sent of the Father, that is as Son
of God, promising the "living water" as the witness of His
coming glory. But I cannot pursue this. Enough if I have
shown how Jesus is presented here, not so much as Son of
Adam, or Abraham, as Son of God.

What follows is equally distinctive, though the force of
the connection may be unperceived save where the life
which connects it is personally enjoyed by us. Hitherto the
burden touching the Son has been, "In Him was *Life.*"
Here He speaks of *Light*: — "I am the Light of the world.
He that followeth me shall not walk in darkness, but shall
have the light of life" (Chap. 8:12). And what a Light it
is! An adulteress taken in the act, with sin confessed,
stands in the light without judgment; while righteous
Pharisees must go out one by one, being convicted by
their own consciences. And the miracle here accomplished
on "the man blind from his birth," illustrates the light-giv-
ing power of this same Son of God. From this point the
word *"truth"* constantly recurs. Faith grows to knowledge; for truth as well as grace had come by Jesus Christ.
The grace saved, quickening to life: the truth sanctified, by
giving light; the Life and the Light both issuing from the
same fountain. He that believed, accepting the "grace,"
obtained eternal life; but he who followed the Pattern, con-
tinuing in the "truth," had light also. So the Lord says
here to "those who believed in Him, If ye continue in
my word, then ye shall know the truth, and the truth shall
make you free" (Chap. 8:31, 32). Faith from the first
gives life; but if we keep the word, light comes, turning
what once was faith into certain knowledge. I may have
come out of the grave of nature, bound hand and foot
with grave-clothes, with a napkin about my face, having life, but no light. Now I have light. "One thing I
know, that whereas I was blind, now I see." And though

rulers who set up to be lights, claiming authority and suc-
cession in the Church, even while saying, "Give God the
glory," may judge the Light-giver and the enlightened,
their judgments cannot rob him whose eyes are opened
of the light of God. In other Gospels blind ones are
healed; but here with the act of healing is added the
witness, "As long as I am in the world, I am the Light of
the world;" for the Spirit would show how light and knowledge, as well as life, are necessary accompaniments of a
true reception of the eternal Word. Need I observe how
all this marks the specific purpose of this Gospel? He that
cannot see this must be blind indeed.

But I will not pursue this, for the general tenor of this
Scripture, little as its depth may be apprehended, needs
no proof. I will therefore only add, that just as the other
Gospels, as they proceed onwards increasingly develop
each its own peculiar view of the Lord Jesus, — as, for
example, St. Matthew, where the chapters preceding the
Passion are full of matters touching the children of the
kingdom, with a testimony of the sin of those who sit in
Moses' seat, so here also, in the corresponding place, the
burden of this Gospel is as distinctly seen in the testimony
of the sending of the Spirit by the Son, and in all that
revelation of the Father's house and heart which is given
only in this Gospel (Chaps. 13-17). This, however, would
lead us where few could follow. I pass therefore to lower
ground, to those scenes which are common to this and to
the other Gospels, to note how different are the points here
dwelt on, how unmistakably they mark the specific view
of Christ, which is here present to us.

Observe then, that in St. John not a word is said of
His apprehensions of the cross, as in the other Gospels.
Here He stands as it were above His sorrows. In St. Luke
(Luke 18:32), He may speak of being "delivered to the
Gentiles, and mocked, and spitefully entreated, and spitted
on." All this is entirely omitted here. Instead of speaking
of His griefs, the Son of the Father, "when He knew that
His hour was come, that He should depart out of this

world unto the Father," is occupied in pouring comfort into His disciples' hearts. He "gives them His peace." He "declares to them the Father's name." "If they loved Him, they would rejoice, because He went to the Father"; for "now is the Son of Man glorified, and God is glorified in Him" (Chap. 14:28; 13:31). And if for a moment, at the recollection that one eating bread with Him should betray Him, His "soul is troubled," and He refers to the betrayal; it is but a passing cloud, only revealing by its contrast the depth and quiet of that heaven of peace which still abode in Him.

It is the same here in the Garden. Life and Light throughout are with Him. St. Luke may show how the Son of Man prepares for His last great conflict; may tell us how He, "who in all points was tempted as we are, yet without sin," said, "Father, if Thou be willing, remove this cup from me;" may show us "an angel strengthening Him," as "in an agony He prays more frevently;" may mark how He seems to seek sympathy from His disciples, while "great drops of blood fall to the ground" (Luke 22:41-44). We look in St. John at the self-same scene; and what a contrast! Not one word of His prayer, or agony, or of an angel strengthening Him: not a word of His sweat, as it were great drops of blood: not a word of His apparent longing for sympathy and companionship in this dark hour. Throughout He is the incarnate Word. "Jesus, knowing all things that should come upon Him, went forth, and said unto them, Whom seek ye? They answered, Jesus of Nazareth. Jesus saith unto them, I am He. As soon as He had said unto them, I am He, they went backward, and fell to the ground." Here, instead of weakness and agony, is power appalling His adversaries. Then again, instead of seeking sympathy from His disciples, here He is seen as possessing and exercising the power to protect them: "Jesus saith, I have told you that I am He. If therefore ye seek me, let these go their way; that the saying might be fulfilled which He spake, Of them which Thou gavest

me I have lost none."° Surely here is both the peace, and
the power, of heaven, even in the bitter cross. He stands as
One from whom no one can take His life, unless He please
to lay it down.

In exact keeping with this, the company of people seen
in St. Luke (Luke 23:27, 28), yielding Him sympathy, "as
they bewailed and lamented Him," and receiving His sympathy in return, as He bids them "weep for themselves," do
not come within the line of vision to which St. John directs
us. An exalted tone, as of the Son of God, runs throughout
the whole. Before Pontius Pilate He is here the calm witness of the "truth," still testifying, "He that is of the truth
heareth my voice." Even on the cross, it is the same.
Abraham's Son may cry, "My God, my God, why hast thou
forsaken me?" (Matt. 27:46). The Servant of God may
also "cry with a loud voice, and give up the ghost" (Mark
15:37). The Son of Man may say, "Father, into Thy hands
I commend my Spirit" (Luke 23:46). But of the Son of
the Father we read, "After this, Jesus knowing that all
things were now accomplished, saith, I thirst." Then "when
He had received the vinegar, He said, It is finished, and
bowed the head, and yielded up the Spirit."° As the eternal
Son He need not "commend Himself" to God. His own
"It is finished," seals with a sufficient witness the full ac-
complishment of His own perfect work. Add to which that
St. John alone omits all record of the darkness, which, as it
had a moral, as well as an historic, bearing, could have no

° Chap. 18:4-9. Such as look closely will notice here many more
interesting particulars. In St. Luke our Lord says, "Father, remove
this cup." In St. Matthew it is "My Father"; because in St. Matthew
it is man in covenant with God that is presented to us. In St. Mark
it is, "Abba, Father."

° Chapter 19:28, 30 — *paredoke to pneuma,* very different from
St. Luke's *exepneusen.* Our authorized version translates both these
very dissimilar expressions by the self-same English words, "He gave
up the ghost"; a rendering which drops the whole force of the contrast, which is clearly intended in the words of the original. The
Vulgate here correctly translates, "tradidit spiritum" in St. John; and
in St. Luke, "exspiravit."

place in the laying down of His life by the eternal Son. Thus it is ever here. The Word is seen made flesh; but the Divine beams forth through the Human everywhere. The cloud is bright with the sun, and the veil even before its rending is transparent to faith at least with heavenly glory.

But enough of what is distinctive. The depth is yet untouched. But what has been said may be sufficient to indicate to God's children what lies before them in this Gospel. The further entrance into it I leave to their prayers and diligence, and to the teachings of that Spirit, whose office it is to take of the things of Christ, and show them to us. I would now, in one or two examples, show how what is distinctive here bears on those who, through grace, are the sons of God in Christ Jesus.

Take then the opening testimony touching the Son, that "in Him was life, and the life was the light of men." What does it teach us who rejoice that "as He is, so are we in this world," as to the nature of that light, which, if He be in us, we too must manifest? It says simply, "The life was the light," — the life, not the profession; "the life was the light of men." There stood One, in a servant's form, in the likeness of sinful flesh, whose life, even while others judged Him, was judging everything, and showing, by its holy contrast, what was in men and what was not, according to God's mind. "The life was the light." It is so yet. The Lord is in us: — "Know ye not that Jesus Christ is in you, except ye be reprobates?" (II Cor. 13:5). And if He be in us, He must yet show Himself by a life, for "in Him is life," and we also must be "light in the Lord" (Eph. 5:8). "I am the light of the world: he that followeth me shall not walk in darkness, but shall have the light of life"; not the light of genius, or of doctrine, but "the light of life"; a light which will make itself felt, even if sinners hate it; which may shine in darkness, and the darkness not comprehend it, but which, misunderstood, slighted, or opposed, has something in it which false professors cannot abide, and from which, sooner or later, they will withdraw themselves. The light of doctrine they can misuse to their own

self-glorification. But the "light of life," a life by self-judgment convincing the world of sin and judgment; a life, by
an hourly preparation for a change, and for the Lord's return, witnessing that we expect Him one day suddenly to
come and judge all things; a life, the foretaste of heaven,
in that its joys are not of nature, which is sorrowful yet
always rejoicing, dying and behold it yet lives; such a life,
just because it is light, and shows pretenses as they are, if
men will not be humbled by it, must be cast out. The wise
of this world shall prove it a delusion, and pious worldlings
lament its injudiciousness, and impious ones mock, and
scoff, and hate it. But through it all, it shall prove it is a
light, by reproving what it comes in contact with, for "all
things are reproved and made manifest by the light" (Eph.
5:13). In the Son of the Father there was life, and "the
life was the light." Let the adopted children see that their
life also is the light of men.

Take another point distinctive here: — "No one hath
seen God at any time: the Only-begotten Son, who is in
the bosom of the Father, He hath revealed Him." How
does this testify of what becomes us as adopted children?
The world knows not God: it cannot see Him: therefore
the children of the Father, even as the Only-begotten Son,
are set here to reveal and recommend Him. If Christ be
in us — for "He cannot be hid" (Mark 7:24) — something
at least of the Father will appear; for where He is, there
the Father that sent Him is seen also. So St. Paul says to
the Corinthians, "Ye are the letter of Christ" (II Cor. 3:3);
ye are they who give Him His character before the world.
He represents you above. You must represent Him here,
and thus reveal the Father, whose image He came to show
to men. If you walk "worthy of God," God is glorified in
you. If otherwise, "the name of God is blasphemed among
the Gentiles through you." For though some have learned
to divide between what is the Church's true position, and
its failing, men do and will judge by what they see. Art
thou a son of God? Then, as the Only-begotten Son revealed Him, so in thy measure must thou also. Would men

learn by thee what God was? This is the test of Christians; this too is the test of true Churches. This it is which, if we understand our calling, compels us to deal in grace; which forbidding us to seize our brother by the throat, saying, Pay me that thou owest, commands us to suffer all things; because God now is dealing in grace, forgiving trespasses, and has set us here to represent that grace, by a life of sacrifice, that His character may be revealed in us. Oh! where is He thus revealed? Is that a revelation of Him, which has hid from men the holy and gracious standard which befits His kingdom; which has made it possible to be zealous for the Church, while careless of His glory; at peace with and honored by her, while not at peace with Him; judging while He is showing grace; in honor where He was rejected; descending to rule this world, instead of with Him waiting for that which is to come? Is this the revelation of the Father? If it be, then He who is without variableness or shadow of turning has indeed changed, since the Only-begotten Son revealed the glory, full of grace and truth.

But I must conclude. For to show how the distinctions in this Gospel bear upon our walk, and illustrate our calling, as children of the Father, would lead me far beyond the limits here permitted to me. And indeed the things here shown are of such a nature, needing to be revealed by the Holy Spirit, that they are better left to be spoken by Him, in His sweet teachings, as He sees we need them. God grudges nothing. He who gave His Son, He whose Spirit is content to dwell in tabernacles, which, though by his workmanship made fair within, are without of badgers' skins, has shown how freely He gives. If we can bear it, all is ours: if we have it not, it is because we cannot bear it. Let us, like John, make our dwelling nigh to that side cleft for us, seeing in the water and blood shed there a pledge of those unsearchable depths of love which still remain, and we may drink our fill of love; and as no lack is there, so surely will there be no grudging. Oh, what depths are here! The heaven and earth were made; and thrones, and dominions, and principalities, and powers, were made also. But the Maker is here before us, made for a season like to us, that we might by Him be changed to bear His image; till, made like Him, His works are wrought in us also, till we by Him are workers of His works to His glory.

I say therefore, Let such as desire to know what becomes them as God's children, ponder well the peculiarities of this Gospel; ponder them as little children, as poor in spirit, diligently using what they have, that they may receive more. "Much food is in the tillage of the poor" (Prov. 13:23): their garden of herbs is small; but diligence gets much food thence, and health can use it all. If we be such "poor" ones, this Gospel will for us produce "much food": then in each peculiarity will some treasure be found by us. Is the Son the "Lamb of God?" We too must be lambs; not swine or dogs, with the mark of the beast, but with the spirit of a dove abiding on us. Has the Son both life and light? The begotten children, like the Only-begotten, must exhibit both life and light also; and though often misunderstood, and unintelligible to carnal and godless men, must show in their ways, because Christ is in them, the living truth of which sabbaths, passovers, and feasts of tabernacles, were but the faint figures. As sons of men they may at times have fears, and doubts, and darkness. But, as sons of the Father, their place is to walk even now as admitted within the veil: calm in trial, strong in weakness, betrayed but not distracted, to the end the unwavering witnesses for the same blessed Truth.

PRAYER

Lord, all things are possible with Thee. Fulfil Thou Thy purpose. Thou hast predestinated us to be conformed to the image of Thy beloved Son. So conform us to Him here, by making us partakers of His cross and resurrection, that like Him we may reveal Thee, and not ourselves, in all our ways. *Amen.*

The Common Testimony

"All these worketh that one and the self-same Spirit" I Cor. 12:11.
"To us there is one Lord Jesus, by whom are all things, and we by Him" I Cor. 8:6.

HITHERTO I HAVE SPOKEN ONLY of the diversities of the Gospels. We have seen that these variations throughout are part of a Divine purpose, the appointed and appropriate means for affording a fuller revelation of the manifold relationships of the One Lord. And though to some this is an offense, as other acts of the same "wise God," to them that are called it is a sure corner-stone.

But from what is distinctive I would now turn to speak of what is common to all the Four Gospels. For if what is peculiar to one or other of them has ever it own purpose, and is instructive as revealing the special experiences of this or that relationship of the One Elect; what is common to all is not less instructive, as showing those experiences which must attend the Head and His members in each and all their relationships. For some things come upon us, as upon Christ, as sons of Abraham, some on us as servants, some as Adam's children, and some as sons of God. But some trials and joys there are which are common to the elect in every relation, which must be our experience, whether as sons of Abraham, or Adam, or as servants, or as sons of God. These experiences, which belong to us in all our relations, are the burden of that testimony which is common to all the Four Gospels.

What is this common witness? Not His birth, not His age, not His baptism, fasting, or transfiguration; but the

111

cross and resurrection, the death of the flesh, the life of the spirit; the sufferings of Christ, and the glory which should follow. Out of countless acts and words of Jesus, death and resurrection is chosen to be the great subject for the common testimony. The Son of Abraham suffers and dies: the Servant of God suffers and dies: the Son of Man suffers and dies: the Son of God suffers and dies. The Son of Abraham rises: the Servant of God rises: the Son of Adam rises: the Son of God rises.

The Church is "in Christ" (Eph. 1:1, 3, 4, 6, 7, etc.). He is the Head, we the members (I Cor. 12:12). He that saith he abideth in Him ought to walk even as He walked (I John 2:6). Other things, therefore, may be doubtful, but this is sure: the cross and resurrection must be ours, if we are His. Other things may vary. One is a prophet; one has tongues; one has knowledge; one the gifts of healing. But as the body is one, and hath many members, so also is Christ, for by one Spirit are we all baptized into One Body. And then, though of all it cannot be said that they preach with Christ, yet of all without any exception it is true that they are "crucified with Him" (Rom. 6:6; Gal. 5:24), of all, that they are "risen with Him" (Col. 2:12, 3:1), of all that they must "suffer with Him, that they may also be glorified together" (Rom. 8:17). It cannot but be so, for "we are no more twain," He in us, and we "in Him."

Would to God this union of Christ and His members were understood. Then the lesson of the cross would not as now so often fall on heavy ears. "In Christ Jesus," — "Surely not in vain, (as another has said), does this language recur so frequently, on so many different occasions. No mere external relation, as being members of the visible body called by His name, exhausts the inwardness of the words, 'in Christ.' It stands there in deep simplicity, yet opening the hidden mystery of union with Christ, and of the reality of our dwelling in Him, and He in us. It is not any unity of will, though worked by Him; no mere conformity of mind, though by Him wrought; no act of faith, casting itself on His mercy; no outward imputation of righteousness; no mere ascription of His perfect obedience in our stead; no being clothed upon, as people speak, with His righteousness; not being looked upon by the Father *as* in Him: none of these things come up to the reality of being '*in Him.*' And why, when Scripture speaks of being '*in* Him,' speak of 'being regarded *as* in Him?' Why, when Scripture speaks of being 'clothed with Him,' speak of having His righteousness cast around us to interpose between our sins and the sight of God? When Scripture talks of realities, why talk of figures? No, there is a reality in this Scripture language, which is not to be exchanged away for any of these substitutions. As we are '*in* Adam,' not merely by the imputation of Adam's sin, but by an actual community of a corrupt nature, derived to us from him by our natural descent from him, so that we have a sad share in him, as having been in him, and being from him, and of him, bone of his bone and flesh of his flesh; so, on the other hand, are we '*in* Christ,' not merely by the imputation of His righteousness, but by an actual, real, spiritual, origin from Him, not physical, but still as real as our descent from Adam. As we are really 'sons of man' by physical birth, so are we as really and as actually 'sons of God' by spiritual birth; sons of man by being born in Adam, sons of God by being members of Him who is the Son of God."

Let us turn then to His cross, not only with the joy of faith, as seeing how for us sin was judged, and man brought nigh to God in Christ Jesus; but looking on it as a thing to be attained to, and as desiring in the Spirit each according to our measure to apprehend what we are apprehended for. I only note the common witness, that therefore which is the elect's common portion, whether as sons of Adam or Abraham, as servants, or as sons of God.

Here is the common testimony. In all the Gospels Christ is betrayed by one, denied by another follower: in all, a disciple is near Him, striving instead of yielding, attempting to escape the cross by a carnal appeal to human energy: in all, He is judged by the Priests, and Scribes, and Elders: in all He is condemned by Pilate, that is the great of this world: in all Barabbas, who was imprisoned for sedition, is preferred before Him: in all He is crucified, and numbered with transgressors: in all He is stripped, and His raiment is taken from Him, and parted among His murderers: in all He dies: in all He has a grave prepared by others: in all He rises, and as risen speaks and walks with men.

As He is, so are we in this world; and though many a step is trod by the elect before he reaches the death of self and resurrection, yet this is our goal, for this we look, this is the end to be pressed to, yea with great longings; "that we may win Christ, and be found in Him; that we may know the power of His resurrection, and the fellowship of His sufferings, being made conformable unto His death, if by any means we may attain to the resurrection from the dead" (Phil. 3:10, 11). And though with us, even as with Him, if Christ be formed in us, there will first be increase in wisdom and stature here: and then a sitting with the doctors, hearing and asking questions, for babes in Christ yet talk with doctors, in a way never repeated after heaven is opened to us — though these steps come first, and baptism, and prayer, and fasting, and temptation, and preaching, and many labors; and many a weary hour with disciples and the men of this world, and many a lonely night when God only is witness to our cries and tears and sighings; and hours of joy too when babes believe, and when our faces shine, and the departed seem very near to us, and we are for a moment transfigured with the light of coming glory — though all this must precede the cross, yet it shall come at last, if only through grace step by step we follow onward whither the Spirit leads us. Little by little, if we walk in the Spirit, the cross is reached, even as little by little, if we walk in the flesh, it will be removed from us.

He who hung there for us reached it not at a step, but by many stages, by common and little and every-day acts of truth and faithfulness; even as they who brought Him to it did so in like manner, by common, little, every-day sins; one because he would sell the truth to gain a little money; others to quench the light which judged them; others, through fear of man, yielding to popular outcry, dreading not to be accounted Caesar's friend; others, as those who pierced Him, simply in the way of trade, without the slightest personal grudge or quarrel with Him. Each in his way, a step at a time, crucifiers and Crucified, reached the cross; they by sparing, He by sacrificing, self in all things. For it could have been avoided. Had He never spoken to strip deceivers bare, had He deserted His post, had He exposed Judas, had He prayed for the legions of angels which wait to serve the elect, had He used the might of this world, had He never called disciples, the cross might have been escaped, and man might have remained, living out his life of Adam, with such things as earth gives, but without a better kingdom. But it could not be so, for He came to do the Father's will, through death to lift man to the place of the Son even in the Father's bosom. So the corn of wheat fell into the ground, and abode not alone, and has sprung up to bear much fruit.

And so with us. If we seek our own, Christ's cross may still be missed. But if like Him we seek in all things to do the Father's will and not our own, content through toil, prayer, and fasting, to follow step by step, then the common witness of the Gospels shall in due time be fulfilled in us also. Some of our brethren who have eaten of our bread shall betray and some deny us; while some with honest love, yet carnal, shall strive if it may be by human energy to save and free us here; and Priests shall sit in judgment on the Lord and His anointed, and the Rulers condemn us that they may be Caesar's friends; and they who fight for freedom even by sedition shall be preferred before us; and we shall be exposed a spectacle to men and angels: and though we may have covered the nakedness of others, ours shall be seen and mocked, while our enemies shall clothe themselves with that they take from us.

Indeed, this shall be seen by all; for though few even of those we love see the elect transfigured and submitting in the garden, all see the bitter cross; it is meant to be seen, to show man's rightful lot, even while it shows the love of

Him who from such dishonor will lift man to everlasting glory. So we shall die, and be laid low, and yet rise, and speak to men in the power of a life which is not of this world; though by nature sons of men, now declared to be the sons of God according to the Spirit of holiness and by the resurrection from the dead. For this was wrought in the Head: it must be therefore the lot of those who through grace grow up to be conformed to Him in all things.

Such is the common witness. The four living creatures, speaking out of the depths of God's sanctuary, here speak but one language. For the veil, whereupon they are wrought, is rent from the top throughout; and, in its rending, their forms must needs be rent also.* Blessed be God that it is so, for until the cherub-covered veil is rent, the way into the holiest cannot be open to us. Till it is rent we stand without in the first tabernacle, still among shadows, the figures of the true. But the four-fold witness is agreed. The veil with its cherubim must be rent. The four living creatures bear but one testimony. And the "three that bear record on earth" — in all a seven-fold witness — "these three also agree in one" (I John 5:8). The Spirit, and the Water, and the Blood, answer from earth to heaven, sealing the same witness of death and resurrection.

Thus answers the Spirit in the Church: "I believe in God the Father Almighty, and in Jesus Christ, His only Son, our Lord; that He was conceived of the Holy Ghost, and born of the Virgin Mary, and suffered under Pontius Pilate; that He was crucified, dead, and buried; that He descended into hell; that He rose again from the dead the third day; that He ascended into heaven, and sitteth at God's right hand, from whence He shall come to judge the quick and the

---

* The veil was covered with cherubims. We read, "Thou shalt make a veil of blue, and purple, and scarlet, and fine-twined linen, of cunning work; with cherubims shall it be made" (Exod. 26:31, and 36:25). This veil, St. Paul expressly tells us, represented "Christ's flesh." (Heb. 10:20). And we are members of His body, "of His flesh, and of His bones" (Eph. 5:30).

dead." Such is the Spirit's witness. Such is our faith touching the Son. Such, therefore, is our faith touching those who in Him are sons also. I believe that they who are sons must be conceived, not of the will of the flesh, nor of the will of man, but of the Holy Spirit. I believe that they must be born, not of the mother of harlots, but of a virgin (II Cor. 11:2; Rev. 19:7), whose name is well called Mary, for she hath known bitterness. I believe that they must suffer; nay more, that for God's true sons there are but few steps between their birth and some suffering. I believe that they must bear the cross, and die, and lie in the grave, and be raised, and in due season ascend to heaven. I believe they must return to earth to judge the quick and the dead, for "the saints shall judge the world"; nay, it is written, "they shall judge angels" (I Cor. 6:2, 3). It is the Spirit that beareth witness, and the Spirit is truth. He that believeth hath in himself the witness. And though some things may vary, this is sure for all God's sons: this is our faith: would that it were our experience also.

The Water speaks the same, as with another seal assuring us of this same truth of death and resurrection. For why are we baptized? "Know ye not," says Paul, "that so many of us as were baptized into Jesus Christ were baptized into His death? We are buried with Him in baptism, wherein also we are risen with Him, through the faith of the operation of God, who hath raised Him from the dead" (Col. 2:12). For the water is a mystic grave: and we do not bury live things but dead things; and our old man is buried there in hope of resurrection. Therefore it is said again, "We are buried with Him by baptism into death, that like as Christ was raised from the dead, even so we should walk in newness of life. For if we have been planted together with Him in the likeness of His death, we shall be also in the likeness of His resurrection" (Rom. 6:3-5). Thus baptism is our profession of death and resurrection: from it Paul can answer, "If the dead rise not, why are we then baptized for the dead?" (I Cor. 15:29). Circumcision told no such story. In that sign of a bygone age, when man in the flesh, the carnal seed of the believer, was taken into covenant, there was only "the putting away of the filth of the flesh" (I Pet. 3:21); for it was yet a trial of the flesh, whether man in the flesh could be cleansed and fitted for the Lord's presence. But now in baptism it is "the putting off of the body of the sins of the flesh" (Col. 2:11). It has been proved that flesh and blood cannot inherit the kingdom: that not "its filth" only must be "put away," but that "the body of sinful flesh," because it is sinful, must be "put off" to gain a better resurrection. Thus does the Water also witness that the elect must die, that our appointed calling is to death and resurrection.

The Blood repeats the same. For as oft as we drink it we do show forth the Lord's death until He come. The corn is bruised, the grape is crushed, to make the bread and wine. And sharing this bread and wine — many kernels and yet one bread, many grapes and yet but one chalice — we represent that common life which is ours when we are bruised that we may be truly one in Christ Jesus. Life is through death; and this is true in Him and in us. So speaks the Blood, even as the Water and the Spirit. Nay more. Brought through the waters, like Noah, the death of the flesh becomes to us far more than mere testimony. Now it is meat also for the elect. In the world before the flood, before resurrection-life is known or reached by us, we feed on the fruits of the earth, those fruits of righteousness, which, whether in Christ or in ourselves, naturally afford man some satisfaction. As yet the death of the creature is no satisfaction to the elect, though God is satisfied, and we are clothed thereby. God's fire may fall and consume the oblation, but we are not partakers with Him. It is otherwise when resurrection-life is apprehended. Then the death of the creature is not only a witness, but it affords us food: the elect also can find satisfaction in it. They too can now rejoice in the giving up of life, and great is the strength which the spiritual man derives from the meat which is thus given to him.*

If these things are so, then have we, who profess to believe, deep cause for humiliation; for while we all proclaim the cross, few of us show faith in it by being crucified by it to the world and the world to us. Another has said, "The boast of our day is that Christ crucified is preached. But is He, even in this one respect, *fully* preached, or the doctrine of the cross fully comprehended? Let the walk of those who make the boast answer. It is not insinuated that such are chargeable with licentiousness or immorality. But are they therefore not chargeable with 'walking after the flesh,' and 'making provision to fulfil its desires?' In the multitude of particulars it is difficult to make a selection.

"But what then is the high regard in which blood, and ancestry, and family connection, are held by some? What is the regard to personal appearance and dress in others? What the attention to ease and comfort, and oft-times profuse expenditure, not to speak of actual luxuries, in the arrangement of the houses, tables, etc., of almost all? Is all this, and a thousand things too numerous to particularize, consistent with reckoning ourselves *dead* as to the old or natural man? Is this what the Scriptures intend by *crucifixion of the flesh?* Alas! full well do many of the professing Christians of our day show that they are but half taught the very doctrine in which they make their boast: that they have but half learned the lesson which even the cross teaches. They have learned that Christ was crucified *for them,* but they have not learned that they are to be 'crucified *with Him*'; or they have found an explanation for this latter expression in the imputation of His death for our justi-

---

* Compare Gen. 1:29, where we read of man's food before the flood, with Gen. 9:3, where the grant of the flesh of beasts is recorded. When God's religion was in the flesh, it was part of the true religion to eat flesh, as in the Offerings, to witness our satisfaction in the death of the creature. Vegetarianism is only one sign among many of the age we live in, when the attempt is, if possible, to blink the curse, and to forget death and resurrection.

fication; a part of the truth, but not the whole; for in vain in this explanation of the words should we seek an answer to the objection which the Apostle anticipated. Indeed, that objection is confirmed by it, for it is nothing else than making the cross the reprieve of the flesh from death. And then when death itself comes to give the refutation to this creed, and to show that the Christian is not saved in the flesh, then is the effect of this half-learned lesson seen.

"Instead of welcoming death as that of which his life has been the anticipation, the execution of that sentence on the flesh, which, since he has known Christ as crucified for him, he has learned in its desert, and has been continually passing on it in mind and spirit, the dying with Christ daily, the 'being planted in the likeness of His death' — instead of being enabled in this view actually to glory in his infirmities, in the weakness, yea, and the dissolution of the flesh, and like the victim found on the arrival of the executioner to have anticipated the end meditated for him, being found of death dead — he is scarcely resigned to die, and impatient of suffering in the flesh. And why? Bacause that truth which the cross of Christ was designed to teach, he never distinctly understood, or rather experienced — namely, that salvation is not in the flesh, but in the Spirit; not *from* death, but *out of* it; not the reinstating of the old nature, but the conferring of a new, by the dying and rising again with Christ."

But this doctrine finds little acceptance. What pleases? "If you wish to please," so said Lord Chesterfield, one who knew the world, "you must make men pleased with themselves: they will then be pleased with you." But the cross is meant to make men displeased with themselves, to humble and abase them. How then can it be so preached as to please all men? A way has been found. Let us say to men, Thank God you are not like others. You hold the true doctrine of salvation by faith in Christ's sufferings. You are not like those deluded creatures who think to be saved by works or feelings. You are not like those Papists, or High-Churchmen, or Dissenters, just as the case may be. Let us thus by implication, while preaching even truth, lay to men's souls the flattering unction that they whom we address are not as other men, and they will be well pleased. And having by us been pleased with themselves, they will be pleased with us in return, and the truth shall seem to have acquired many friends.

But let the true cross be brought before men, the death of self in all its forms, the end of righteousness and strength and will as sons of Adam; let us show that participation with the sufferings of Christ into which the Holy Spirit leads us — the deep joy there is even in the midst of outward sorrows in the putting off of old Adam — the life in things that are unseen, in righteousness, joy, and peace, which takes away even the desire to have something or to be something here; let this be preached in life and word, and we shall find the offence of the cross remains, now as of old a stumblingblock, not least to those who thank God that they are "not as other men."

The fact is that we live in a day when the cross as it bears upon our life is very generally condemned as the exploded folly of a less enlightened age. It is possible, so a popular preacher has lately expressed it, *"to make the best of both worlds."* The Christian now can show the heathen how to get more out of this world than they knew before; not resurrection, but power in the flesh; not the Holy Spirit, but learning and wealth; not Christ at God's right hand, and we in Him, but discoveries, blessings, and institutions here. Christ and His Apostles lost this world. They could not, or did not, make the best of both; but we in wiser days can gain both worlds. So the aim is a walk of faith, so as not to exclude a walk of sight; heaven perhaps some day, but at all events a better home, a safer resting-place on this side death.

The old Church said, Christ suffered, and His saints must suffer. The new gospel is, Christ died in the flesh that we may live in it. Mortifications therefore, and crosses, and fastings, are a mistake. The lot of the Head and the members may differ very widely. It is true He suffered and died,

but we know that cross was for us: why should we bear
what He once bore for us? Thus is the cross which con-
demns the flesh preached as its reprieve, and as the excuse
for carnal and careless walking. Oh cunning lie of the
devil, to cut us off from Christ, to make Him and His members not one body; as if we could indeed be His, and miss
the cross; as if the improvement of the fallen creature, and
not its death, were our appointed calling. Such a religion,
"the way of Cain" (Jude 11), cultivation of the creature
instead of death, fruits of the earth offered as if neither sin
nor the curse were working in it — such a religion will
generally please, though even here, if God has the best,
the devotee will not escape censure from some who boast
to be spiritual. But let there be blood, a life poured out —
"for the blood is the life" — let there be the yielding to
death of what is animal in us — let there be self-judgment,
intellect, judged, this is rank superstition, treason against
Him who made or permitted the creature to be what we
now see it.

We are not in Eden, but in a groaning world: explain it
as we will, death is here; a curse works in us. But our religion shall forget both the sin that has caused this, and its
judgment; good fruits of the fallen creature shall be a sufficient offering. So thought Cain; so think his children; but
their offering lacks the flame. And though some of the most
beautiful exhibitions of good fruits, now as of old, are to be
seen on Cain's altars; fruits most sweet in their true place,
as an adjunct to the blood of the lamb, and as such accepted; for in the Meat-offering God will have fruits offered
where there has first been the blood of the Burnt-offering;
yet are Cain and his seed angry with their brothers who
confess the curse by a death of the flesh in hope of resurrection.

And even true Christians stumble here. Like Martha we
say, "Lord, if Thou hadst been here, my brother had not
died." We think if Christ were with us, death and sorrow
would not come; if He were here, we should escape the
curse. To such thoughts His answer is, "I am the resurrec-

tion; believest thou this?" She saith unto Him, "Yea, Lord, I believe that Thou art the Christ, the Son of God." Christ says, "I am the resurrection; believest thou *this?*" and we reply, "Yea, Lord, Thou art the Christ"; a good confession, but not the answer to the Lord's question. If we really believed Him to be "the resurrection," we should understand that there must first be death, for without death there can be no resurrection. Thus, "I am the resurrection," would answer our thought, "Lord, if Thou hadst been here, my brother had not died": but with Martha we can only say, "Yea, Lord, we believe that Thou art the Christ, the Son of God." "And when she had said this, she went her way, and called Mary"; a secret consciousness that the subject was beyond her leads her to call others; even as to this hour, "I am the resurrection," the Church's life in Christ, her blessed privileges through death and resurrection, often drive God's children away from Christ to brethren, to conceal the lack of communion which makes His words too high and painful to us.

But I must conclude. Happy are they to whom the cross of Christ is not a rock of offense, but a most sure cornerstone, who in the ancient faith of saints, still believing those oft-repeated words — *"He was born, He suffered, He died, He rose"* — can yet be content to add as the conclusion of such a creed, *"I look for the resurrection of the dead, and the life of the world to come."* Time was when "with great power the Church bore witness to the resurrection," for of "the multitude of them that believed, none said that aught that he possessed was his own, but they had all things common." Then "as many as were possessors of lands and houses sold them, and distribution was made to every man, as he had need" (Acts 4:33-35).

And whence all this? He whom they had walked with upon the earth, He who loved them even unto death, was cast out of this world. They knew He was Lord of heaven: and they longed to be like Him, and to be with Him; sharing with Him His portion here, as sacrifices for others; sharing with Him His blessed hope. But the path was hard for flesh and blood: false brethren made it harder. Soon the first love waxed cold. And soon as saints forgot their hope, they began to improve the world that is, that they might improve their own lot in it. Thus, the Church's temptation, even as her Lord's, has ever been to anticipate her future glory in a fallen world, to seek a home in a creation yet tainted with the curse. Let her remember sackcloth is her clothing here (Rev. 11:3). Christ's crown and purple robe were the gift not of His Father, but of His murderers. If the Church be crowned and in purple in this world, let her see to it, and ask — Is she truly adorned by these things, or is she mocked by them?

"Let us therefore, as many as be perfect, be thus minded; and if in anything ye be otherwise minded, God shall reveal even this unto you. Nevertheless whereto we have already attained, let us walk by the same rule, let us mind the same thing. Brethren, be followers together of me, and mark them which walk so as ye have us for an ensample. For many walk, of whom I have told you often, and now tell you even weeping, that they are the enemies of the cross of Christ: whose end is destruction, whose God is their belly, and whose glory is in their shame, who mind earthly things. For our conversation is in heaven, from whence we look for the Saviour, the Lord Jesus Christ; who shall change our vile body, that it may be fashioned like unto His glorious body, according to the working whereby He is able even to subdue all things unto Himself" (Phil. 3:15-21).

Yet one word. These pages may fall into the hands of some who as yet are not at peace with God. To such, even as to believers, my testimony is of Christ Jesus. Him hath God exalted to be a Saviour. Our real misery is that we do not know either ourselves or God. Of ourselves we have good thoughts; of Him, hard thoughts. Christ's life and death meet this: they bring proof that there is no hope for man in himself — every hope for him in God his Saviour. God, however, as He is the true God, can deal only with realities. He occupies Himself with what really is. We must therefore come to Him as we really are. Come to Him, pretending to be what you are not, and there can be no true peace. For God will not deal with you on the ground of pretenses. Come to Him as you really are: God will go with you to the very bottom of your misery, and, because He is God, has grace which will meet your every need. Trust Him, and you have peace. Doubt Him, and trust yourself, and you can have no peace, though every ordinance in the world may have been observed by you. "He that believeth on the Son of God hath the witness in himself. He that believeth not God hath made Him a liar, because he believeth not the witness which God gave of His Son. And this is the witness, that God hath given to us eternal life, and this life is in His Son" (I John 5:10, 11).

Praise ye the Lord. Praise God in His sanctuary: praise Him in the firmament of His power. Praise Him for His mighty acts: praise Him according to His excellent greatness. Praise Him with the sound of the trumpet: praise Him with the psaltery and harp. Praise Him with the timbrel and dance: praise Him with stringed instruments and organs. Praise Him upon the loud cymbals: praise Him upon the high-sounding cymbals. Let everything that hath breath praise the Lord. Praise ye the Lord.

Index

OF

THE TEXTS PECULIAR TO EACH GOSPEL